P9-EDE-896

À TABLE

À TABLE

RECIPES FOR COOKING + EATING THE FRENCH WAY

REBEKAH PEPPLER

Photographs by Joann Pai

CHRONICLE BOOKS

SAN FRANCISCO

Featured on this page:
Kouign-Amann, page 252.

Text copyright © 2021 by REBEKAH PEPPLER.
Photographs copyright © 2021 by JOANN PAI.

All rights reserved. No part of this book may be reproduced
in any form without written permission from the publisher.

Library of Congress Cataloging-in-Publication Data

Names: Peppler, Rebekah, author. | Pai, Joann, photographer.
Title: À table : recipes for cooking + eating the French way /
   Rebekah Peppler ; photographs by Joann Pai.
Description: San Francisco : Chronicle Books, 2021. |
   Includes index.
Identifiers: LCCN 2020036444 | ISBN 9781797202235
   (hardcover) | ISBN 9781797204543 (ebook)
Subjects: LCSH: Cooking, French.
Classification: LCC TX719 .P464 2021 | DDC 641.5944--dc23
LC record available at https://lccn.loc.gov/2020036444

MIX
Paper from
responsible sources
FSC™ C008047
FSC
www.fsc.org

Prop and food styling by REBEKAH PEPPLER.
Additional editing by BLAKE MACKAY.

The photographer would like to thank her parents for
passing down their passion for food, her husband for
his love and support, and JKE for forcing her to move
to Paris to pursue her dreams.

Design by LIZZIE VAUGHAN.
Typeset in Maison Neue and Flatline.

10 9 8 7 6 5 4 3 2 1

Amer Dit Picon is a registered trademark of Maison De La Vie,
Ltd.; Angostura bitters is a registered trademark of Angostura
International Limited; ARCHTHE is a registered trademark of
Jung Joon; Bonal is a registered trademark of Dolin Company
France; Bonne Maman is a registered trademark of Andros
Société en Nom Collectif; Bragg is a registered trademark
of Bragg Live Food Products, LLC; Brightland is a registered
trademark of Brightland Incorporated; Campari is a registered
trademark of Davide Campari Milano S.P.A.; Cheez-It is a
registered trademark of Kellogg North America Company;
China-China is a registered trademark of SAS BIGALLET
société par actions simplifiée; Cointreau is a registered
trademark of Cointreau Société Par Actions Simplifiée; Cool
Whip is a registered trademark of Kraft Foods Group Brands
LLC; Curious Elixirs is a registered trademark of True Business
LLC; Dubonnet is a registered trademark of Dubonnet Wine
Corporation; Fever-Tree is a registered trademark of Fevertree
Limited Limited Company; Fog Linen Work is a registered
trademark of notebooks.ltd; Grand Marnier is a registered
trademark of Marnier-Lapostolle Bisquit Société Anonyme;
Häagen-Dazs is a registered trademark of HDIP, Inc.; Heinz is
a registered trademark of H.J. Heinz US Brands LLC; IKEA is
a registered trademark of Inter-Ikea Systems B.V. Corporation
by Assignment Netherlands Olof Palmestraa; Jacobsen salt
is a registered trademark of Jacobsen LLC; Kerrygold butter
is a registered trademark of Ornua Co-Operative; Kin is a
registered trademark of Kin Social Tonics, Inc.; La Croix is a
registered trademark of Everfresh Beverages, Inc; Lactaid is
a registered trademark of Johnson & Johnson Corporation;
Lillet Blanc is a registered trademark of Societe Lillet Freres;
Maille is a registered trademark of Unilever N.V. Corporation;
Maldon is a registered trademark of Maldon Crystal Salt
Company; Microplane is a registered trademark of Grace
Manufacturing Inc.; Nikki Chasin is a registered trademark
of Nikki Chasin LLC; Nonino amaro is a registered trademark
of Nonino Distillatori S.R.L.; Party City is a registered
trademark of Party City Corporation; Pedialyte is a registered
trademark of Abbott Laboratories; Peychaud's is a registered
trademark of Sazerac Brands, LLC; Pineapple Collaborative
is a registered trademark of Pineapple DC, LLC; Plugrà is
a registered trademark of Dairy Farmers of America, Inc;
Post-it is a registered trademark of 3M Company; Président
is a registered trademark of B.S.A. Société Anonyme à
Directoire et Conseil de Surveillance; Punt e Mes is a
registered trademark of Fratelli Branca Distillerie S.R.L.; Q
Tonic is a registered trademark of Q Tonic, LLC; Ratatouille
is a registered trademark of Pixar Corporation California;
Schweppes is a registered trademark of Dr Pepper/Seven Up,
Inc.; Seedlip is a registered trademark of Seedlip Ltd limited
company; Suze French aperitif is a registered trademark of
Pernod Ricard, SA société anonyme; Thin Mints is a registered
trademark of Girl Scouts of The United States of America
Congressionally Chartered Non-Profit Corporation; Williams-
Sonoma is a registered trademark of Williams-Sonoma, Inc.

Chronicle books and gifts are available at special quantity
discounts to corporations, professional associations, literacy
programs, and other organizations. For details and discount
information, please contact our premiums department at
corporatesales@chroniclebooks.com
or at 1-800-759-0190.

Chronicle Books LLC
680 Second Street
San Francisco, California 94107
www.chroniclebooks.com

DEDICATION

"ON NE NAÎT PAS FEMME: ON LE DEVIENT."*

In gratitude to all the women who have shaped and continue
to shape my becoming, but especially the first.
I love you, Mom.

"ONE IS NOT BORN, BUT RATHER BECOMES, A WOMAN."*

En remerciant toutes les femmes qui ont façonné et continuent
de façonner mon avenir, mais surtout la première.
Je t'aime, maman.

*—SIMONE DE BEAUVOIR

INTRODUCTION

Evening in France has a distinctive kind of magic. If you've been, you know. There is often conversation and golden light; there are drinks, small bites, and friends meeting to celebrate the start of the evening, seemingly every night.

At my house, appetites and hearts opened, we tuck eight bodies around a table that comfortably seats six and pass plates and bottles and stories back and forth until only dried rings of wine and heels of bread remain. By dessert, emptied platters have been relegated to the floor, making room for something sweet and a dealer's-choice approach to digestion: bottles of amaro or whiskey or vermouth and a bowl of ice.

I host nights like this weekly in my apartment in Paris's 18th arrondissement. Often they fall on Sunday, teetering at that transitional cusp between one week's wind-down and the start of the next. Contrary to pretty much everything anyone has said about dinnertime in France, I set the start at a bright-eyed 6 p.m. This gives me the morning at the market and the afternoon to cook, while ensuring that even with the très French gap between start time and actual arrival, there will be plenty of sunset in which to throw open the balcony doors and have a drink before gathering à table.

Guests are a rotating cast. There are friends who live in the neighboring arrondissements, friends and family visiting from thousands of miles away, friends of friends, lovers, potential lovers. There are people who know where the coats go (bedroom, corner chair, next to the balcony door for that inevitable break in the night when someone runs out for a smoke to see the Eiffel Tower sparkling and, en masse, we desert our dessert and grab said outerwear). There are those who know which drawer holds the extra candles and those uninitiated yet quick to learn that I don't leave empty glasses empty.

À Table takes the elegant, sexy, sparkling charm that is a French evening and gives you the tools to gather this way in your own home, wherever that may be and whether you're cooking for a group of eight, a family of two, or your current self and your future leftover-loving self with leftovers in mind.

Today more than ever it seems we get together like this: often and intimately. Gone is the old way of entertaining, the import placed on pressed linens, floral arrangements, babysitters, and days of preparation. Through practice and necessity, a deep awareness of limitations in time, budget, and space has been cultivated. A tiny kitchen or lack of separate dining room or mismatched plates doesn't stop us.

This book is a dive into gathering folks in this modern way, through the special lens of the French table. It champions a night ending in crumb-covered laps and stained shirts. The food—delicious, always—is served alongside good vibes and engaged conversation, whether it be about the failings of the Democratic establishment or the new Christine and the Queens album.

Before I moved to Paris, I often hosted in Brooklyn and Los Angeles. The kitchens and markets and cultural norms have shifted, but the energy crosses the border with ease.

In France, there's an added—and basically mandatory—l'heure de l'apéritif (the subject of my first book!). This hour ushers in the night, wherein connection and simple beauty best technique and complicated flavor, and where a weekday evening can flow into a decidedly un-puritanical bedtime. The rituals and customs around eating, drinking, and gathering in France have long been romanticized, and for good reason TBH. No matter how enchanted an evening in France may be, its magic can be translated with some simple, elegant steps. The recipes, remarques, and anecdotes in these pages aim to show you how to turn this fantasy into a reality.

In France, no matter where you live, your age, your ethnicity, your socioeconomic background, when you call people to come together around a table, you say the same thing: à table!, which translates as "to the table!" English speakers may mispronounce, of course, but the phonetic English holds up just as well: a table.

However you say it, *À Table* is about gathering over food and drink, coaxing the fantastical from the real, and unabashedly sharing it with your people.

AUX AMOUREUX ET AUX RÊVEURS
(TO THE LOVERS AND DREAMERS),

—RP

A NOTE ON ITALICS

For this book, I chose to take a closer and more active look at how English language texts use italics to demarcate and, thus, "other" non-English words. This book, written by an English speaker and published by an English-speaking American publishing house, includes French words and phrases throughout the text in an effort to inform, provide color, or deepen the reader's understanding of my personal experience in the country I call home. While a translation and/or explanation for these inclusions is often provided with an eye toward clarity, *À Table* does not follow what has been the standard practice of italicizing non-English words.

This shift may require a small lift from English-speaking readers who, after years of conditioning, need a moment to readjust to a style that doesn't frame English as the dominant language. To readers who have a working knowledge of French, I hope this stylistic shift furthers and provides fluidity to your experience of reading two languages side by side. To those who rightfully question why I'm taking this particular stand with French—a language and culture that has often and readily contributed to the colonization and othering of cultures and peoples around the world—I say this: We can only start where we are.

MODERN FRENCH PANTRY, ABRÉGÉ

Regardless of kitchen size—and believe me, the Parisians have a lock on tiny—a well-stocked pantry is key for any cook, especially if you're feeding people on the regular. While the French still tend to head to the market or their favorite corner shop for fresh ingredients daily, the following is an abbreviated (abrégé) list of items that I keep around to provide the building blocks to any meal, the French way. Most are easy to find regardless of where your kitchen is, and all make it into more than a few recipes in this book. Mind you, I'm not the biggest fan of "pantry sections" in cookbooks—don't tell me how to live my (pantry) life!—so I'll keep the list short and the info tight, just like your final pantry should be.

Bacon

The French word for bacon is "lard." For centuries, a salt-cured and smoked piece of lard was often the only meat available in winter, hence the English word "larder," meaning pantry. French bacon is either smoked (fumé) or unsmoked (. . . non fumé) and generally sold in large slabs or little rectangular lardons rather than slices. To make lardons yourself, cut thick-cut or slab bacon crosswise into ¼-inch [6 mm] strips.

Brined Things

Cornichons

Few things bring me greater joy than a good pickle. Cornichons—pickled mini gherkins—make their way onto the French table from apéro through the meal, and many thanks for that.

Capers

Capers are small flower buds that are dried in the sun, then either brined or packed in salt to draw out their inherent bitterness. They're salty and tangy and perfect.

Olives

To name a favorite French olive would be as impossible a task as naming a favorite French wine. A few favorites such as Picholine, Lucques, and Niçoise—as well as the Italian queen of buttery green olives, the Castelvetrano—are used throughout the pages of this book. Explore them, then get thee to any French market and keep exploring.

Butter

On a photo shoot in Paris and working at dinnertime, I was happily making my way through a baguette and a package of salted butter—slice, barely spread, eat, repeat. When I looked up, my assistant was staring at me with huge eyes. In a voice I can only describe as awe-filled, she said, "I've never seen anyone eat butter like cheese before." I was very proud to have broadened her horizons that day.

The French take their butter seriously. There are two types the French (and this book) use most often: salted (demi-sel) and unsalted (doux). There's also a subcategory of salted butter with big crystals (gros cristaux) that's best for simply setting on the table with a baguette. And then there are butters flavored with additions such as seaweed, paprika, yuzu, and vanilla bean, which are excellent as gifts but a bit fussy for daily needs. Salted or not, European butter has a higher fat content than American butter, which equals a richer taste and is the reason I call for it in the recipes in this book. You can, of course, use non-European butters if your store doesn't carry them or your budget doesn't allow, but know that the flavors are going to be a touch mellowed. When I'm using European butter in America, I most often reach for Plugrá, Échiré, Kerrygold, or Président. In France, I love Beillevaire and Bordier for snacking, and a supermarket brand with blue wrapping for cooking and baking (DM me and I'll find out the name).

In *À Table*, most recipes call for unsalted European butter, but feel free to swap in salted without adjusting any seasonings if the amount of butter is under 3 tablespoons. If over, adjust your seasoning.

Cheese

Cheese is a daily part of life in France, and lucky for us all really, there are so many of them. Most are meant to be eaten just as is, but there are a few to also use in cooking, such as Comté—Comté + Sesame Twists (page 71), Croque Madame (page 169), French Onion Soup with Cognac (page 177), and Gratin Dauphinois (page 229). If you can't find this creamy, nutty, highly snackable Alpine cheese from the Jura region of eastern France, or eat it all before you get to cooking (been there), sub Emmental or Gruyère. Other cheeses important to the recipes in this book (and life) are Parmesan, Camembert, and something blue such as fourme d'Ambert (a milder French blue), Bleu d'Auvergne (medium-bodied, balanced), or Roquefort (a bold cheese for the bold among us). For a cheese board or life in general, I recommend seeking out an aged Cantal (the texture and flavor are kind of like Cheddar because it's made the way Cheddar is made . . . but French Cantal was being made 1,200 years before English Cheddar was a thing), crémeux de Bourgogne (a buttery triple-crème from Burgundy), and tomme de Savoie (a musky, semisoft, rustic cow's milk from the Rhône-Alpes). Oh, and Mimolette.

Chocolate

It's an understatement to say that there are excellent chocolates made in France (and Belgium and Switzerland). I always have a few bars for tucking onto an assiette sucrée (page 270) or for afternoon snacking. I favor 55 percent to 70 percent cacao solids for baking, both for flavor and because if you get north of the 70 percent mark, the chocolate has higher acidity and can alter a recipe's outcome. While *technically* not chocolate, I do use and eat and love white chocolate. Buy some to make Chocolate Pudding, but French (page 260) and snack on the extras. Any chocolate keeps best between 65°F and 70°F [18°C and 21°C], kept away from direct sunlight and protected from moisture, so basically any cool, dark place, but not the refrigerator. If it's summer, tightly wrapped in the refrigerator is OK.

Citrus

During citrus season, I keep big bowls of clementines, mandarins, and kumquats on my counter and pretend I'm in Southern California. Lemons and oranges are on hand year-round for drinks as well as everyday cooking and eating. But oranges seem to be France's daily favorite. You can find machines that freshly squeeze orange juice to order all over Paris, and it's a damn joy. Replicate by squeezing your own citrus fresh—by machine or hand—for any of the recipes in these pages. The small effort is worth the difference in flavor.

Condiments Both Sweet and Savory

Mustards

You need two mustards, always, in the house: a smooth Dijon and a crunchy whole grain. To keep things properly French, buy Maille, which is widely available in the States these days.

Preserves

The French love their morning tartine, which is a fancy name for a length of baguette served with salted butter and preserves. As a non-breakfast person myself, I can still attest to the glory of a morning tartine. But preserves—apricot jam in the case of *À Table*— have a place outside the breakfast table as well: (My First) French (Girlfriend's) Apple Tart (page 246) and Pork Chops with Kale (page 138), par exemple.

Harissa

Not a traditional French ingredient but essential to the new French pantry, harissa is a chile paste originally from Tunisia. It ranges from hot to mild and varies from brand to brand. Try a few and find what you love, or do what I do and keep three different jars and tubes in the refrigerator.

Crème Fraîche, Milk, and Other Dairy

I've learned the hard way to read French dairy labels—they love to ferment things, and have you ever accidently tried buttermilk or kefir in your coffee? Here's a quick guide:

Milk

Milk, called lait frais, comes in entier (whole), demi-écrémé (2 percent), and écrémé (skim). You can get it pasteurized (pasteurisé) or raw (cru). The French are also really into shelf-stable milk; I am not.

Buttermilk

Buttermilk is labeled as lait fermenté, lait ribot, or lait caillé.

Crème fraîche

Crème fraîche is a little thicker and a little less sour than American sour cream. While you should be able to find crème fraîche in most major and some non-major American grocery stores, sub in sour cream if you can't. The French also have something called crème crue, which is raw cream that has never been heated and no bacteria cultures have been added. It's normally sold out of big white buckets at small local markets in Normandy (and sometimes Paris), and if you get the chance to try it, buy a quart and any fruit that's in season and spend some time alone with them. I often use crème crue to make the Tomato Tart (page 166).

Heavy whipping cream

Labeled as is crème liquide, crème fluide, or crème entière. If you're in France and want whipping cream for Strawberries + Crème (page 241), make sure you don't buy crème légère, which is low-fat and contains thickeners and . . . will not whip. A cream needs to have at least 30 percent fat to whip, so if you're in the United States, you're good: American heavy cream hovers around a standard 36 percent.

Extra-Virgin Olive Oil

I have a friend who started the California-based olive oil company Brightland a few years back, and through her I learned the value (both culinary and environmental) of actually good, sustainably sourced olive oil. Because not all budgets allow for using very good oil for both cooking and drizzling, I recommend keeping one relatively inexpensive oil on hand for cooking (heating up oil negates some of its nuances) and another

LA COMPAGNIE BRETONNE
conserves fines de la mer

SARDINES
à l'huile d'olive Bio

Pêche fraîche de saison
Travaillées à la main
Fabriquées en Bretagne

Conserverie familiale Jean-François Furic

"Nuri" Brand
SPICED PORTUGUESE SARDINES
IN PURE OLIVE OIL (HOT SAUCE) CHILE PEPPER
(PIRI-PIRI) CARROT, CUCUMBER, LAUREL,
CLOVE and PEPPER - CORN, SALT

NET WEIGHT 3.16 OZ. (90 GRAMS)

filets de maquereaux
marinés au vin blanc et aux aromates

la belle-iloise

CALLE EL TATO tapas gourmet

Serie ORO

SARDINILLAS EN ACEITE DE OLIVA 20/25 PIEZAS
Petites sardines à l'huile d'olive 20/25 pièces

PICAS
PORTUGUESAS
EM AZEITE DE OLIVEIRA
Luças
SINCE 1896
LUÇAS & Cᴬ Lᴰᴬ
MATOSINHOS - PORTUGAL

PRODUTO DE PORTUGAL

SARDINHAS
PORTUGUESAS EM
AZEITE VIRGEM EXTRA
Luças
Brand
PRODUCT OF PORTUGAL
LUÇAS & Cᴬ Lᴰᴬ
MATOSINHOS-PORTUGAL

AZEITE VIRGEM EXTRA
CASA DE
S. MIGUEL
100% PURO

NET WT. 120g (4.2oz)

sardines   à l'huile végétale

LES DÉESSES

SARDINHAS
PORTUGUESAS EM AZEITE DE OLIVEIRA E TOMATE

PRODUTO DE PORTUGAL

Luças
SINCE 1896
LUÇAS & Cᴬ Lᴰᴬ
MATOSINHOS - PORTUGAL

SARDINHAS
PORTUGUESAS EM AZEITE DE OLIVEIRA E PIRI-PIRI

PRODUTO DE PORTUGAL

Luças
Brand
SINCE 1896
LUÇAS & Cᴬ Lᴰᴬ
MATOSINHOS-PORTUGAL

LA COMPAGNIE BRETONNE
conserves fines de la mer

SARDINES
à l'huile d'olive Bio

Pêche fraîche de saison
Travaillées à la main
Fabriquées en Bretagne

Conserverie familiale Jean-François Furic

high-quality oil for salads and finishing. Keep oils in a cool, dark place and use enough to replenish often.

Flours

Any recipe in this book that calls for flour was developed with American all-purpose flour. It doesn't make my trips through customs easy, but I do it for you. In case you're in France and not devoting 5 pounds [2.5 kg] of your carry-on to flour on a regular basis, Type 65 is the closest to American all-purpose. While not used in the pages of this book, for future reference, T45 and T55 are close enough to American cake or pastry flour, T80 for light whole wheat, T110 for whole wheat, and T150 for dark whole wheat.

Salt, Pepper, and Piment d'Espelette

Salt

There are two main salts that I use in my kitchen: fine sea salt and flaky sea salt. You could substitute kosher salt for the fine sea salt, but they're not exactly the same, so keep that in mind as you season. Everyone knows by now, but flaky sea salt is so good. Irreplaceable. I use it to finish most things savory or sweet. Maldon or Jacobsen are both excellent. And, since we're in the *French* pantry over here, fleur de sel—delicate, fine, and harvested by hand—is an ingredient to add to your larder. The best fleur de sel is from Guérande in western France.

Pepper

Both black and white pepper should be used without ration throughout life and *À Table*. I buy both of mine whole and grind them fresh. If you want only one pepper grinder in the house, fill it with black and get your white pre-ground (taste it before using to make sure it's still fresh and flavorful).

Piment d'Espelette

A chile from France's Basque country, piment d'Espelette is lightly spiced and robustly flavored. Find it in powdered and paste form at specialty shops or online. If you really need to substitute, use the best hot paprika you can find.

Tinned Things

Good anchovies

Pantry anchovies are packed in either oil or salt. For oil-packed anchovies, use them straight from the jar and store in the refrigerator after opening. For salt-packed, soak the anchovies in cool water or milk for 10 to 15 minutes. Once soft, insert a finger in the center of the anchovy and slide it down the length of the spine to open up the anchovy. Pull out the backbone, take off any fins, and rinse under cool water.

Tuna

Good tuna packed in good oil is one of the pantry's great pleasures, full stop. With a little mayo and pickle, it's lunch. Tucked into a sandwich with eggs, potatoes, and harissa, it's Casse-Croûte Tunisian (page 156). With a bowl of greens, beans, and olives, it's Niçoise (for a Crowd) (page 155), a.k.a. dinner.

Vinegars

I confess that I love a wild and weird vinegar gift, but I always have the following vinegars on hand, usually with a second bottle tucked away as a backup too:

White wine vinegar

Mild, versatile, delicate in flavor.

Red wine vinegar

Sharply acidic with a stronger grape flavor than white wine vinegar. If you're ever deciding between red and white wine vinegar, ask yourself what type of wine you want to drink with that food and roll with it.

Apple cider vinegar

Fruity and a bit sour. I get my cider vinegar from Normandy. In America, ACV used to be all Heinz and Bragg, but now you have gorgeous (looking and tasting) stuff from brands like Pineapple Collaborative.

Sherry vinegar

Made in Spain, deeply flavored, nutty, and oxidized. Love it.

Wine and Other Booze

Not just for drinking (but also for drinking), wine and other alcohols appear in a lot of French dishes, and so you'll see wine and spirits listed as an ingredient throughout *À Table*. As ever, cook with wine you would also drink, not just so you can drink what you don't use, but also because quality of ingredients matter! Tell your aunts: There's no such thing as "cooking wine." More thoughts on wine on page 53.

DOM IN THE KITCHEN, SUB IN THE DINING ROOM: A PHILOSOPHY FOR PLEASURE IN HOSTING

Before the start of any dinner party, I'm going to top you. I'll tell you when and where to show up, exactly what and exactly whom to bring with you. If I'm feeling extra or it's a celebratory night, I'll broad-strokes tell you what to wear. In the kitchen leading up to your arrival, I set up the night with you specifically in mind. I choose the recipes; I know what tools and techniques I want to use and I know how to use them. I dictate the food you'll be eating and the space you'll enter, with the knowledge that the moment you arrive, I switch.

Here, in the hallway as I trade coat for cocktail and send you into the dining room to apéro, I serve you. I make sure your wine and water stay full. If you're gluten-free or meat-free or have an allergy, there's something special, just for you, my queen. I anticipate if and when you want something and make it happen—often before you ask but always, always if you do. Near the end of the night, I have something sweet I know you'll like: a bottle of something special to try, maybe, poured into the glass you prefer.

Regardless of your interest in power dynamics in *other* rooms of the house, this philosophy for hosting is well within your wheelhouse. A few rules:

BE DECISIVE

This is clearly important before guests arrive and you're deciding on things such as start time and recipes and lighting-scape, but decisiveness is just as important after the guests have arrived and you've switched into the sub role. You're still in charge—as all subs are—it just looks a little different. For example, in nice Parisian weather we all crowd onto the long, narrow balcony for apéro, and it's my role to (kindly) move everyone inside when dinner is on the table—easy in rain or winter, more a seduction in fair weather.

KNOW YOUR GUESTS

Empathy goes a long way, in life as well as during a successful dinner party. Get and stay attuned to your guests. Set terms by asking questions in advance. If you've invited people who don't know each other, introduce them with a connective talking point so they don't have to start with the weather. If someone isn't drinking that night for LITERALLY WHATEVER REASON, THEY DON'T HAVE TO EXPLAIN THEMSELVES, have something special and non-boozy ready for them, both when they walk in the door and to drink throughout the night. Sparkling water, nonalcoholic cocktails, a special soda: all great options (see page 60 for more). If you know someone has social anxiety, invite them over a bit early for some one-on-one time before any crowd amasses.

UNABASHEDLY PLAY THE "MY HOUSE, MY RULES" CARD

I'm a firm believer in keeping people and thus the party energy around the table, which means I start cleaning only after every single person leaves. The moment people start to get up from the table to clean en masse is the moment the magic of the night breaks—don't let it. If you must, at least make the cleanup part of the experience. Open a bottle of good Champagne or digestif, turn up the music, be cool when someone inevitably breaks a glass.

BE CLEAR WITH YOUR OWN NEEDS

The vibe of a dinner party starts with the inevitable *what can I bring* text. Know what you want and make it easy to source. If you say wine and you're actually hoping for a specific type (white, red, natural), state that clearly and text the name—and a dropped pin—of a good wine shop that's close to their or your home. If it's ice, see page 59. If it's chips or olives or saucisson or whatever prepackaged snackable thing you need for apéro, reserve that ask for your most on-time friend. If you say nothing, mean it and also have something on hand that can house flowers.

BEST-LAID PLANS

When you invite someone over, you have the best of intentions for their enjoyment, in dinner or otherwise. What you don't have is control over them. To wit, you also can't control the weather, a person's mood, or—if you're inviting more than one person—the energy they each bring and how those energies interact. This isn't to say you can't plan and adapt and offer moments along the way, but you cannot control the party, not really. If you want total control, have a night in alone.

BEFORE

PRE-DINNER
DRINKS + SNACKS

BEFORE

Apéritifs

---

*REMARQUE

Snacks

*REMARQUE

APÉRITIFS

CHAUD COMME

For 1

1 ounce [30 ml] blanc vermouth

3 or 4 dashes orange bitters

3 ounces [90 ml] dry sparkling wine

1 ounce [30 ml] soda water

1 large orange wheel

3 big green olives

One of the first dirty things I learned to say in French (after, of course Christina Aguilera's flawless rendition of voulez-vous coucher avec moi ce soir) was je suis chaude comme une baraque à frites. Translated literally, it means "I am hot like a French fry hut," but in slang it means you're horny as hell. This spritz is for those hottest of days, where you're as sweaty (or as turned on) as you would be should you find yourself, say, inside a poorly ventilated shack frying French fries.

Fill a wineglass with ice, then add the vermouth and bitters. Top with the sparkling wine and soda water. Add the orange wheel and olives directly into the glass and serve.

PRE-DINNER ARMAGNAC

For 1

1¼ ounces [35 ml] Armagnac

½ ounce [15 ml] dry vermouth

¼ ounce [7.5 ml] fresh lemon juice

¼ ounce [7.5 ml] 1:1 simple syrup (see Note)

Sparkling water, for topping

Bold, rich, and aromatic, Armagnac is France's "first" brandy, produced in the Armagnac region in Gascony and often served after a meal. This recipe lightens the moonlight spirit to sunset hours with the addition of vermouth, lemon juice, and simple syrup, and lowers the ABV with sparkling water. Serve over ice and alongside a snack (both literally and colloquially).

In a shaker filled with ice, combine the Armagnac, vermouth, lemon juice, and simple syrup. Cover and shake vigorously. Strain into an ice-filled lowball glass, top with sparkling water, and serve.

Note

To make 1:1 simple syrup, combine 1 cup [240 ml] of water with 1 cup [200 g] of sugar in a medium saucepan over medium heat. Bring just to a simmer, turn the heat to low, and cook just until the sugar dissolves. Remove from the heat and set aside to cool to room temperature. Use immediately or store in a covered container in the refrigerator for up to 1 month.

232

For 1

1¼ ounces [35 ml] red
bitter such as Campari or
Cappelletti

1¼ ounces [35 ml] fresh
grapefruit juice

1 ounce [30 ml] fino sherry

¼ ounce [7.5 ml] 1:1 simple
syrup (see Note, page 36)

Sparkling water, for topping

Grapefruit wedge, for
garnish

While I'm not advocating everyone have a house cocktail, I
also am. Named after the number of steps I climb up to get
to my apartment in Paris, this combination of dry sherry, red
bitter, and fresh grapefruit juice (pictured on page 33) is
mine—but I'm a good sharer. Prep the grapefruit garnish
in advance. Depending on your guest count, double, triple,
quadruple, and pre-batch the bitter-grapefruit-fino-syrup
mix. When the buzzer rings, shake to order, and the cocktails
will be ready to drink by the time each person makes it up
however many stairs you've got.

In a shaker filled with ice, combine the red bitter, grapefruit
juice, sherry, and simple syrup. Cover and shake vigorously.
Strain into an ice-filled lowball glass, top with sparkling water
and a grapefruit wedge, and serve.

KIR PISCINE

For 1

Scant ½ ounce [15 ml]
crème de cassis

5 ounces [150 ml] dry white
wine, such as Aligoté or
Muscadet

Someone needs to say it: Late summer in Paris is terrible. Sure, it has its blue sky and green grass and ample excuses for day drinking, but Haussmann's old, gorgeous buildings were not built with climate change in mind. Air conditioners aren't really a thing in France, the garbage union goes on strike as often as the transportation union (so, a lot), and French deodorant is . . . ineffective. Luckily there are piscines. The French word for swimming pool is also used to describe adding a lot of ice to drinks, both to cool them down and lengthen the time it takes to finish them, say, by the pool. This particular piscine (pictured on page 84) takes the standard kir—a most classic French apéritif made with black currant liqueur and dry white wine—and adds ice to personal preference. The frozen addition both cools and extends, teaches and delights.

Pour the crème de cassis into a wineglass and top with the wine. Serve with ice cubes.

C&T

For 1

2 ounces [60 ml] Calvados

4 to 5 ounces [120 to
150 ml] dry tonic water,
chilled

Note
An altogether different drink, but if you swap in ginger beer for the tonic and garnish with a lime wedge, you probably won't be mad at it.

A G&T is the drink of Thibault, my best friend in Paris and my backup French husband. Because there's nothing I love more than offering people I love something they love, this classic cocktail has been flowing out of my bar since the day we met.

On an autumn trip to Normandy, I discovered a regional take that trades Calvados—a local French apple brandy—for the gin and is often served chilled without ice. The outcome of not diluting your drink with ice is that it is both refreshing and bracing (keep some cubes nearby if you find you need to tone it down a bit). When I hand Thibault a C&T for apéro, he rolls his eyes but also drinks the whole thing, so.

In a chilled highball glass, add the Calvados and top with tonic. Serve cold.

SUZE SOUR

For 1

1¼ ounces [35 ml] Suze

1 ounce [30 ml] 1:1 simple syrup (see Note, page 36)

1 ounce [30 ml] fresh lemon juice

½ ounce [15 ml] fresh lime juice

1 small egg white

Note

The dry shake is a key technique whenever you're making drinks with egg. First, use a vigorous shake sans ice to facilitate foaming, then add cubes for a second shake to chill and dilute. The technique is effective, but since egg proteins expand and raise the pressure inside the tin, it can also get a bit messy; keep a towel nearby and a firm grip on your shaker.

Suze—a classic, gentian-based French apéritif—is very yellow and very bitter, and the bottle is objectively very pretty on your bar. Two types of citrus, simple syrup, and an egg white come together here to smooth Suze's edges and create a bright, silky, and light drink, with just enough bitterness to make you think, *Campari's for lightweights, I'm a Suze drinker now.*

In a shaker, combine the Suze, simple syrup, lemon juice, and lime juice. Add the egg white, cover, and dry-shake (see Note) for 15 seconds. Add ice, cover, and shake vigorously for another 15 seconds. Strain into a coupe glass and serve.

BAMBOO TONIC

For 1

1 ounce [30 ml] fino sherry

1 ounce [30 ml] dry vermouth

¼ ounce [7.5 ml] green olive brine

1 dash Angostura bitters

1 dash orange bitters

Dry tonic water, for topping

Green olives, for garnish

The classic Bamboo cocktail—created in the 1890s at the Grand Hotel in Yokohama, Japan, by German bartender Louis Eppinger—is equal parts sherry and vermouth stirred with ice and a few dashes each of Angostura and orange bitters, served up. Definitely make it. This recipe lengthens the rich flavor of the original with bittersweet tonic. I add olive brine because the salinity works and also I would drink olive brine straight.

In a Collins glass filled with ice, combine the sherry and vermouth. Top with the olive brine and bitters; add enough tonic water to fill the glass, finish with olives, and serve.

DIMANCHE

For 1

1½ ounces [45 ml] Lillet Blanc

1½ ounces [45 ml] dry vermouth

½ ounce [15 ml] orange liqueur, such as Grand Marnier or Cointreau

3 dashes orange bitters

1 ounce [30 ml] dry sparkling wine

1 orange peel

My friends in Paris tend toward a loose (read: freelance) sense of "the workweek," but Sundays are still my favorite day to have people over. I dodge granny carts and wicker baskets at one of the big outdoor markets in the morning, cook in the afternoon, throw a long, full dinner, and am still in bed before 11 p.m. While lovely on les dimanches, of course, the Dimanche is just as good on any of the other six calendar days.

In a mixing glass or shaker filled with ice, combine the Lillet, vermouth, orange liqueur, and orange bitters. Stir with a cocktail stirrer for 15 seconds, until the cocktail is very cold. Strain into an ice-filled lowball glass; top with sparkling wine. Hold the orange peel by its long edges, skin facing down into the glass. Pinch the peel to express the citrus oils, then discard the orange peel and serve.

AMARO OLD-FASHIONED

For 1

½ teaspoon turbinado sugar

3 dashes Angostura bitters

2 ounces [60 ml] amaro, such as China-China or Nonino

Orange peel, for garnish

Maraschino cherries, for garnish

Whenever I visit my hometown in Wisconsin, the first thing I drink is my stepdad Mike's whiskey old-fashioned. It's sweet, strong, and, when paired with a game of cribbage, tastes like home. It's also an extremely potent way to start a night. In Paris, I make them for friends when we know we're in for a rowdier evening. But when seeking something lighter in ABV but not lighter in flavor, amaro replaces whiskey. I'm partial to France's China-China amaro for this variation, but any amaro that veers sweet and herbal will play nicely.

Add the sugar, bitters, and 2 teaspoons of water to the bottom of a lowball glass. Stir until the sugar is dissolved, then fill the glass with ice and pour in the amaro. Stir with a cocktail stirrer for 15 seconds, until the cocktail is very cold. Finish with the orange wedge and cherries and serve.

50/50

For 1

1½ ounces [45 ml] gin

1½ ounces [45 ml] dry vermouth

2 dashes Angostura or orange bitters (optional)

An excessive amount of green olives (seriously, go ham at the olive bar)

Note

Lillet Blanc subs in nicely for the vermouth if you're drinking 50/50s before 4 p.m.

The majority of my apéritif recipes—both in my books and served in my home—don't include any hard alcohol for a variety of reasons (most of them hangover related). But I'm a believer that an at-home martini is one of life's great pleasures. This variation (pictured on page 63) employs slightly less gin, to the tune of about half, which is an excellent excuse to drink two without worrying about sending ridiculous texts. I like the addition of bitters, but they're ancillary. Nonnegotiable are the olives, served in the glass and on the side in a quantity that one might describe as a snack.

In a mixing glass or shaker filled with ice, combine the gin, vermouth, and bitters. Stir with a cocktail stirrer for 15 seconds, until the cocktail is very cold. Strain into a chilled cocktail glass or an ice-filled lowball glass. Add one to three olives to the glass, and serve with more olives on the side.

THE OTHER 50/50

For 1

1½ ounces [45 ml] blanc vermouth

1½ ounces [45 ml] dry vermouth

There's the 50/50 martini (above) and then there's The Other 50/50 (pictured on page 65). This might be my favorite drink in the whole world, and the first woman to batch it and put it on tap will be my wife. It moonlights in French as the moitié-moitié (half-half) and is traditionally made with equal parts sweet and dry vermouth. This version swaps in blanc vermouth for the sweet red stuff, but if you have a dope sweet vermouth on hand, pour freely.

In a mixing glass or shaker filled with ice, combine the blanc and dry vermouths. Stir with a cocktail stirrer for 15 seconds, until the cocktail is very cold. Strain into a chilled cocktail glass or an ice-filled lowball glass and serve.

CHAMBÉRY CASSIS

For 1

3 ounces [90 ml] dry
vermouth

½ ounce [15 ml] fresh
lemon juice

½ ounce [15 ml] crème de
cassis

Soda water, for topping

Currant sprig, for garnish
(optional)

Hemingway was a supreme ass, but he did offer a few
worthwhile things: succinct prose, a model for how to actually
work in Paris, and a nod to this cocktail in *A Moveable Feast*.

In a Collins glass filled with ice, combine the vermouth, lemon
juice, and crème de cassis. Top with soda water, garnish with
currants, if desired, and serve.

APÉRITIF SCORPION BOWLS

You know scorpion bowls: communally shared, heavily boozed and sugared, hangovers biding their time inside every straw. These updated Apéritif Scorpion Bowls keep the fun and ditch the sting (ugh). All follow the main tenets of apéritif: low ABV, low effort, high reward. Serve these in that ceramic bowl covered in hula girls your mom found at a garage sale, a regular large bowl, or a pitcher. If you're taking them to go, these recipes all conveniently fit into a recently emptied 750 ml bottle.

APÉRITIF SCORPION BOWL UN

For a crowd

12 ounces [360 ml] amaro, chilled

12 ounces [360 ml] sweet vermouth, chilled

6 to 8 dashes Angostura bitters

4 lemon peels

Sparkling water, chilled, for topping

In a punch bowl or pitcher, combine the amaro, sweet vermouth, and bitters. Working one by one, hold the lemon peels by their long edges with the peel facing down into the bowl. Pinch the peel to express the citrus oils and drop the peel into the bowl. Serve in ice-filled punch or lowball glasses and top each drink with sparkling water just before serving.

For a party of 1

2 ounces [60 ml] amaro, chilled

2 ounces [60 ml] sweet vermouth, chilled

2 dashes Angostura bitters

Sparkling water, for topping

Lemon peel

In an ice-filled punch or lowball glass, combine the amaro, sweet vermouth, and bitters. Top with sparkling water. Hold the lemon peel by its long edges with the peel facing down into the glass. Pinch the peel to express the citrus oils, drop the peel into the glass, and serve.

APÉRITIF SCORPION BOWL DEUX

For a crowd

8 ounces [240 ml] Lillet Blanc, chilled

8 ounces [240 ml] fino sherry, chilled

6 ounces [180 ml] fresh grapefruit juice

4 ounces [120 ml] 1:1 simple syrup (see Note, page 36)

8 dashes Angostura bitters

In a punch bowl or pitcher, combine the Lillet, sherry, grapefruit juice, simple syrup, and bitters. Stir to combine and serve in ice-filled punch or lowball glasses.

For a party of 1

1 ounce [30 m] Lillet Blanc, chilled

1 ounce [30 ml] fino sherry, chilled

¾ ounce [22.5 ml] fresh grapefruit juice

½ ounce [15 ml] 1:1 simple syrup (see Note, page 36)

2 dashes Angostura bitters

In a shaker filled with ice, combine the Lillet, sherry, grapefruit juice, simple syrup, and bitters. Cover and shake vigorously. Strain into an ice-filled punch or lowball glass and serve.

ON HOUSE WINE
AND WINE IN GENERAL

I am here to help us all make the leap with regard to House Wine. You know the stuff—likely served at a French or Italian or Greek restaurant, always options of red and white, sometimes rosé too. It's inexpensive, served by the squatty glass or carafe, and very satisfying. But House Wine, really, is just a concept and one that you can and should bring home to *your* house.

Since my home doesn't have a wine cellar or refrigerator, I designate the small cabinet next to my circuit breaker as storage for eight to ten bottles of House Wine. I keep those same bottles of inexpensive, highly drinkable, glou-glou, natural wines (see page 54) in rotation, skewing the mix of red, white, and rosé more heavily in one direction or the other depending on the season. And I'm loyal-ish with them. I'll keep replenishing the same bottles until I find something I like better, and then I phase that one in. Which means if you're my friend and come to my house regularly, you're often drinking the same thing or a variation on the theme you had last time.

To wit, I keep a bonus bottle of sparkling wine in my refrigerator, because life comes at you fast and there should always be cold bubbles ready for a toast, celebratory or otherwise. And I also usually have a few special bottles, often imbued with quite a bit more funk. Those I break out for the right drinking buddy, but the beauty of having House Wine go-tos is they're all delicious sure bets no matter who's coming over (if those that are coming over drink wine) or which day of the week it is when you want to pour yourself a glass.

Maintaining a small collection of House Wine takes care of apéros and dinners, not to mention third dates that turn into seventy-two hours of not leaving the house (strong recommend). This way of keeping wine has also given me way more confidence when going about the business of buying and serving wine.

Yes, living in Paris offers the obvious perk of ready access to good, affordable, interesting, and drinkable wine. (Also, unpasteurized dairy, universal health care, and efficient train travel.) But while there's a lot of good wine in France, there's also a lot of crap wine. And regardless of location, sorting through it all can be daunting, especially when you're stocking up or bringing a bottle to a friend who is "into wine." In my head it often sounded a lot like this: *There are so many types! So many well-designed labels! Have I had this bottle before? Did I like it? Is Riesling always sweet?* (No! But maybe try one from Austria.) *Is Chardonnay gauche?* (Absolutely not, but go for French over Californian). This is when you can and should call in the professionals, namely your friendly neighborhood wine shop.

Having someone to talk to who (a) knows about wine, (b) is getting paid to talk about it—and, hyper important here—(c) actively learns and helps you learn and expand on what you like is the surest way I've found to go from *I like to drink wine* to *I like to drink xyz wine*. It's also a solid way to support local businesses. In Paris, I have three: the shop by my house, the shop by my therapist, and the really awesome little shop that's a little too far from my house but walkable if I limit myself to three bottles or fewer. In each, I've gotten to know the people who work there, and in turn, they've gotten to know me, my tastes, and my budget. Speaking of budget, most wine shops will happily knock off 10 percent or offer the whole "buy eleven bottles, get the twelfth free" deal if you buy a case. Extra incentive for the starter pack on House Wine.

Friendly reminder: You don't need to know wine lingo or pretend you know more than you do to talk with the staff in your chosen shop. If you feel intimidated, that shop sucks; choose a different one.

Then, drink. Might I even suggest a dinner party with other people who drink so you can try a bunch of different bottles in one night? Taste is of course subjective, and you can't know what you like without trying—and you might actively dislike some. That's great! You're very allowed to not like some things, even if they're the cool wines. In many ways, interesting and thoughtfully made wine is more accessible than ever, and I suggest being open to it surprising and delighting you, but drink what tastes good in your mouth. Note the bad with the good and report back to your aforesaid wine person.

Now that you know what you like, share the wealth. I often answer a pre–dinner party *what can I bring* text with a quick *vin stp* ("wine please"). At this point, my friends either know what they like or bring something they know I'll like. It hasn't always been like that. So you might follow your own *vin stp* with a *let me know if you want a bottle rec!* or a *medium-bodied rosé would be perfect!*

A lot of my friends in Paris will tell you they didn't know much about wine before I started serving and chattering excitedly about my own favorite bottles and producers whenever they came over. Whether you're hosting or bringing a bottle, the key to transferring that light mania is a slow pour of enthusiasm, gratitude, and really, truly not being a snob about it. Rather, be extra generous with favorite bottles and let the fun, engaged, wine-soaked evening ensue. Soon enough friends will snap photos of labels they love, and then, full circle, people will bring bottles you'll be taking photos of to add to your House Wine cabinet.

A SMALLER REMARQUE ON NATURAL WINE

My House Wines are almost exclusively natural wines. As with all matters of subjective taste, this is a personal preference and by no means a mandate. France produces, uh, a lot of wine in both the "conventional" and "natural" styles of winemaking. "Natural" is the catchall term for, broadly, low-intervention wines made from grapes grown without pesticides or added sugars, and little to no sulfur. To complicate things a bit, while natural wine often shares a label with organic wines, not all natural wines are organic and not all organic wines are natural. Fun! Regardless, the level of care and hands-off approach to natural wine results in bottles that are vibrant, distinctive, and quite special. Insecure people like to scoff at trends, but I subscribe to the natural wine ethos unabashedly.

Bubbles

Sparkling wine is a clear choice for apéro hour or a housewarming gift, but I've also hosted many a dinner where bubbles were the drink of choice from start to finish. There are a few different ways wine gets a sparkle, most commonly méthode champenoise (traditional method), méthode ancestrale (ancestral method), and charmat (tank method).

In the traditional method (used to make Champagne and Cava), wine is fermented and then transferred to bottles with more yeast and sugar (dosage) for a second fermentation. It's during this second fermentation that the bubbles are formed and trapped in the bottles. The bottles are aged (sometimes for many years), stored at a downward angle, and turned often so all the dead yeast particles move into the neck of the bottle and can later be disgorged.

A meme but also true: Legally, only wines made in the Champagne region of France can be labeled "Champagne." There are big houses in Champagne that tend to buy their grapes and then there are grower Champagnes, which are made with grapes grown by the winemakers themselves. Guess which I prefer. In general, however, if you go with a good house, it's likely both delicious and expensive. It's also probably on the drier side. The Champagne you find on shelves is largely labeled under an iteration of "brut." From driest down, it goes brut nature, extra brut, then brut. If you happen across a bottle with the words "sec," "demi-sec," or "sweet," they're going have a higher dosage (sugar level).

Bottles of pétillant naturel or pét-nat use varying versions of the méthode ancestrale. The natural winemaking technique—which experts say predates the traditional method—garners characteristically delicate effervescence and some great, funky, lower-in-ABV bottles, often at a much lower price point than Champagne. Wine is fermented, bottled while it still has residual sugar, and continues to ferment in the bottle—without any additives. Most pét-nat isn't disgorged, so don't be surprised if what you pour into the glass looks a little cloudy. While pét-nats can be made anywhere in the world, the movement started in France.

Step outside the French border and you'll find Prosecco and Lambrusco—both Italian and both made in the charmat method, in which the second fermentation is carried out in pressurized tanks, generating bubbles more quickly than the traditional method, before being bottled.

White

For the most part it's simple: White wine grapes create white wine. But just as there are exceptions to the rules in the French language, so too are there in wine. Whether you press a white or red grape, you get white juice, and so it follows that white wine can be made with red grapes—but this is mostly found in sparkling wines. To avoid any color, the grapes (whether white or red) are crushed and then immediately pressed to remove the skins and seeds, resulting in little if any maceration during fermentation.

White grape varieties are plentiful—talk to your wine person! A few French favorites: Chenins and Muscadet from the Loire, wines made from Chardonnay (Chablis), Aligoté from Burgundy, and Riesling from Alsace.

Skin Contact

Skin-contact wines, sometimes called orange wines, have their traditional roots in Georgia, Slovenia, and Northeast Italy and are made with white grapes that are macerated with their skins to infuse them with more body, aroma, and tannins. Basically, they are white wines made like red wines and vary in color from very light gold to deep orange, depending on how much time the wine had contact with the skins. Many are fantastic and often a little weird, and you should definitely drink them. In France, the Jura in particular has embraced orange wines, and they're excellent.

Rosé

Rosé is also made like a red wine, using red wine grapes macerated with the skins for a relatively short span of time. There's also the saignée method, which basically amounts to a portion of juices being removed during a red wine fermentation to create a higher skin-to-juice ratio, resulting in a deeper-hued red wine. The early-exit pink juice is then fermented on its own as rosé. This method is sometimes used in Provence (although the better bottles tend to shy away from it). As my friend and wine writer extraordinaire Megan Krigbaum sagaciously said, "Everyone is trying to get a slice of the pie that Provence baked." She's right, as refreshingly easy to drink in the sun as Provençal pinks are, there's now a world of rosés to choose from. If you come to my place in spring or summer, you'll likely find a few bottles of the aforementioned Provençal pie alongside a Tavel (a darker style of rosé from the Tavel region of the Southern Rhône) as well as something Italian from Puglia and Campania because they're killing the rosato game right now.

Red

Both the color and tannins of red wine come from grape skins. Bordeaux, Burgundy, and the Rhône have long been red wine darlings, but regions like the Loire (Chinon, for example), Beaujolais, and Languedoc in the south make some lovely, pas cher (less pricey) reds. Another tip: Look for reds labeled as vins de soif (literally "wines of thirst," meaning thirst quenching)—they're ideal with a light chill and served year-round. A win-win in House Wine.

ON FROZEN WATER

Plenty has been written on ice for the professional bar. Treatises on clarity, freshness, and tools to mold, hand-carve, and brand cubes abound. While I too have strong opinions on ice for your gathering, they boil down to this: You should have it and it should be fresh. If you don't have freezer space, ask someone to bring it.

Ice not only plays a role in pre-dinner cocktail hour but also is a supporting player throughout the meal. Use it to keep extra wine chilled in sinks or tubs or buckets on the balcony, place it under platters of oysters and shellfish, or serve alongside a bottle of digestif and a jumble of pretty glassware.

In drinks, ice does two important things: chills and dilutes. Experts say you'll want to choose the right ice for the job, which will depend on how you're chilling (stirring or shaking) and what you're diluting. For me, the "right" ice and what I used to develop the drink recipes in this book is the standard 1-inch [2.5 cm] cube. You can shake with them, serve over them, or place them in a dish towel and crush them. If you're a fan of a big rock, invest in one of those trays too (just don't stir a cocktail with them; they melt too slowly to properly cool the drink).

I don't particularly mind cloudy ice. It crushes more easily, and if your guests complain about cloudy ice, get less douchey friends. That said, if you're looking to get very clear, bubble-free ice, boil a bunch of water and pour it—still hot—into trays before freezing. If you're deploying this particular method, choose a silicone tray over plastic for obvious reasons.

A SMALLER REMARQUE ON WHEN YOUR HOST ASKS YOU TO BRING ICE

My freezer is the size of two pints of ice cream and an eye mask, so if you're invited to my house, there's a high chance that the response to *What can I bring?* is ice. Hold your cringes and let me climb up on that proverbial high horse: I've invited you to my home; you know the size of my refrigerator (small) and the size of my freezer (smaller); I'm shopping and cooking and setting the stage for your hopefully very lovely evening to come. Please, please, for the love of Juliette Binoche, stop at the corner store for ice. And if you have to go out of your way, do that.

If you ever happen to be in Paris en route chez moi, just go to the Franprix on Rue d'Orsel. Text me—I'll tell you exactly how to find the ice there (it's saved in a note on my phone). When you walk in my door, I'll have a cocktail ready to be mixed with said ice, wine waiting to be chilled, and snacks to help you forget the outlandish ordeal you went through to purchase chunks of frozen water.

ON NOT DRINKING

Considering the content in these pages, you'll be unsurprised to learn that I drink. Except for when I don't. Whether for a night or month or year, a chosen, temporary bout of abstinence or simply drinking less has become a common practice in my friend group and my generation and beyond for the past few years. With that in mind, I'm always prepared for someone to show up to a dinner and not be drinking—whether or not they're sober. While there are loads of diverse reasons behind the phrase *I'm not drinking,* none of them is actually any of your business. What is your business is to make sure your guests feel as comfortable and unilaterally taken care of when you're breaking out the good sparkling water as when you're breaking out the good Champagne. Here are some things to keep on hand for the nondrinking drinkers among us, and a few ways to use them:

Sparkling water
Get the good stuff that comes in big glass bottles and get a lot of it. Also, La Croix Pamplemousse because it may be basic but it's also damn good.

Still water
Get the good stuff that comes in big glass bottles for the nondrinkers who prefer eau plate (still) over eau pétillante (sparkling).

Tonic water
Unless you're in Europe, skip Schweppes (which is overly sweet in the United States) and seek out tonic from Fever-Tree, Q Tonic, and other smaller brands doing big things. Pour it out of the can or bottle into a grown-up glass. Add a Meyer lemon or grapefruit wedge, maybe a metal or paper straw if you're into that sort of thing.

Ginger beer
Get a really strong and spicy one and serve with a big squeeze of lime and some fresh mint.

Verjus
Sweet-tart verjus is made from the pressed juice of unripened grapes and comes in both red (richer and earthier) and white (milder and crisper). Often used in cooking, it's also wildly refreshing over ice and comes with the bonus of letting you open a bottle for your guests just as you would a bottle of wine. Serve solo or add a splash of bubbly water and a citrus peel. Store opened verjus recorked and in the refrigerator for up to 3 months.

Nonalcoholic spirits

There's a plethora of very dope NA spirits in gorgeous bottles out there right now. Brands like Seedlip, Kin, and Curious Elixirs are great, and I'm sure many more are on the market to discover. Seek them out, keep them on the bar next to your bourbon, and pour them neat or over ice or with a splash of soda, as you would any of the other spirited spirits on your bar. Don't make a big deal about it.

Bitters

Know: Most bitters DO HAVE ALCOHOL IN THEM. It's a small amount and very well diluted in, say a bitters and soda, but it's there, so please make sure whoever you're making a drink for is OK with that. Add to a nice glass with sparkling water and a squeeze of citrus. Angostura, Peychaud's, and orange bitters are used in many of the drinks in this book, but for something NA I like to pull out more esoteric flavors, such as persimmon, celery, rhubarb, or maple.

SOME NA MIXED-DRINK IDEAS TO GET YOU STARTED

* Combine ½ ounce [15 ml] simple syrup (see Note, page 36), 1 ounce [30 ml] fresh lemon juice, 1 ounce [30 ml] white verjus, a tiny pinch of flaky sea salt, and a few dashes of bitters (optional) in a lowball glass. Top with ice and cold tonic water; stir to combine. Garnish with a lemon wedge or twist.

* Cut a lime into four pieces and add to a lowball glass. Coarsely chop a ½-inch [12 mm] piece of fresh ginger and add along with 8 fresh mint leaves; muddle everything together. Add ice and top with equal parts ginger beer and sparkling water.

* Combine the peels from 3 limes and 3 lemons with ¾ cup [150 g] granulated sugar in a bowl or container and muddle everything together. Cover and set aside for at least 1 hour (or up to 24 hours). Juice the peeled limes and lemons and add them to the sugar mixture. Cover and shake until the sugar dissolves. Strain through a fine-mesh sieve to remove the citrus peels. This base will keep, covered, in the refrigerator for up to 1 month. To serve, add 1 ounce [30 ml] to an ice-filled glass and top with sparkling water or tonic.

SNACKS

SNACK MIX

**Serves however
many you want
to serve**

Comté cheese, cut into long
pieces

Small saucissons or sliced
saucisson

Potato chips

Mixed olives

Cornichons, halved
lengthwise

Oil-cured anchovies

Piment d'Espelette

Living in France means the rest of Europe is close. This snack mix combines the best of French snacking with the genius that is Spanish pintxos. I've omitted measurements because you know yourself and your guests best. Have a potato chip lover coming over? Add more chips or a mix of varieties. Know that your friends aren't going to appreciate those oil-cured anchovies? Add another type of cheese or sausage—or eat them all yourself. Honor the French-Spanish crossover here and serve with a good vermouth or a vermouth cocktail such as The Other 50/50 (page 45), and don't skip the sprinkle of piment d'Espelette—it ties the whole plate together.

Combine all the snacks on a plate and sprinkle with piment d'Espelette. Serve with toothpicks for easy snacking.

The Other 50/50 | page 45

ROASTED LEMONS + OLIVES

Serves 6 to 8

1 medium lemon

1 pound [455 g] mixed olives, such as Cerignola, Castelvetrano, and Picholine

4 fresh thyme sprigs

2 tablespoons extra-virgin olive oil

¼ teaspoon red pepper flakes

Freshly ground black pepper

On my goddaughter's first trip to visit me in Paris, she took her notebook and pen outside on the balcony and sat wrapped in a blanket drawing the Eiffel Tower and "taking some alone time." It marked the moment that I realized her mother—my best friend since pastry school—and I had become old and perhaps uncool to the next generation, as we sat inside drinking Champagne and eating these olives while talking about things no six-year-old finds interesting. It's a treasured memory memorialized in the drawing on a Post-it that I straight-up stole and framed . . . sorry, Peri.

Preheat the oven to 425°F [220°C].

Thinly slice three-quarters of the lemon into rounds, remove the seeds, and cut into half-moons. Reserve the remaining quarter lemon.

On a rimmed baking sheet or ceramic baking dish, drizzle the lemon slices, olives, and thyme sprigs with the oil. Sprinkle with red pepper flakes and toss to coat; season with black pepper. Roast, tossing occasionally, until the lemons start to caramelize and the mixture is very fragrant, 10 to 15 minutes. Squeeze the remaining quarter lemon over the mixture and use a wooden spoon to gently scrape up any caramelized bits. Serve warm or at room temperature.

OLIVES WITH SAUCISSON

Serves 4 to 6

⅓ cup [80 ml] extra-virgin olive oil

1 cup [160 g] assorted olives, such as Niçoise or Picholine, lightly smashed

3 garlic cloves, smashed

1 lemon peel

1 teaspoon chopped fresh rosemary, plus 2 fresh rosemary sprigs

1 teaspoon chopped fresh thyme, plus 2 fresh thyme sprigs

¼ teaspoon coriander seeds

¼ teaspoon whole black peppercorns

4 ounces [115 g] saucisson sec, very thinly sliced into rounds

Crusty bread, for serving

The French craft of charcuterie began by name in the fifteenth century, marked on storefronts that specialized in the preparation of pig and offal in a time when shop owners weren't allowed to sell uncooked pork. The word "charcuterie," while beautiful to say, is cuttingly straightforward in its translation: from the French words "chair" (flesh) and "cuit" (cooked).

Saucisson sec is one of the more versatile players within the French charcuterie canon, varying by region across the country. Any dry-cured saucisson works here, whether a simple combination of pork and salt or with add-ins like spices, truffles, or nuts. I like the pure stuff, but choose what *you* like and make sure to serve with crusty bread to dredge up the infused oil.

In a small saucepan over medium heat, combine the oil, olives, garlic, lemon peel, chopped rosemary and sprigs, chopped thyme and sprigs, coriander, and peppercorns. Heat, stirring occasionally, until the garlic is golden around the edges, 5 to 7 minutes. Add the sliced saucisson and cook, stirring, for 1 minute more. Pour the whole mixture, including the oil, into a serving bowl; serve warm with toothpicks and crusty bread for dipping.

COMTÉ + SESAME TWISTS

Makes 32 twists

One 14-ounce [400 g] package all-butter puff pastry

1½ cups [120 g] grated Comté cheese

2 tablespoons sesame seeds

1 large egg, lightly beaten

Flaky sea salt

I was in a tiny butcher shop in Burgundy buying pork chops when I saw them: twisty, buttery, cheesy, crunchy prepackaged puff pastry sticks that gave me un coup de cœur. Literally translated to "a hit or shock to the heart," this phrase describes an instant, intense crush for something. (For people, the French often use the equally evocative term "lightning strike," un coup de foudre, meaning love at first sight.) My crush came home with me right away, and I haven't been able to find that particular brand since. So I wrote this recipe and wish you a lifetime of happiness with her.

Preheat the oven to 400°F [200°C]. Line two baking sheets with parchment paper.

Transfer the puff pastry to a lightly floured surface, and roll into a 20-by-10-inch [50 by 25 cm] rectangle (about ⅛ inch [4 mm] thick). Sprinkle the Comté and sesame seeds on one long half of the dough rectangle, leaving a ¼-inch [6 mm] border around the edges. Fold the other half over the cheese-and-sesame filling. Cut the dough crosswise into 32 strips (each about ⅔ by 5 inches [17 mm by 12 cm]). Transfer the strips to the prepared baking sheets and, working with one strip at a time, brush lightly with the beaten egg. Twist each strip and sprinkle with salt. Bake until deeply golden brown, 18 to 25 minutes. Serve warm or transfer to a cooling rack to cool completely, about 15 minutes.

FIG + BLACK OLIVE TWISTS

Makes 32 twists

½ cup [90 g] dried figs, stemmed and quartered

⅓ cup [80 ml] dry vermouth

½ cup [70 g] pitted kalamata olives

½ lemon, zested and juiced

1 garlic clove, grated on a Microplane

1 teaspoon salted capers, rinsed and drained

¼ cup [60 ml] extra-virgin olive oil

Freshly ground black pepper

One 14-ounce [400 g] package all-butter puff pastry

1 large egg, lightly beaten

Note
Make the fig and black olive tapenade in advance, if you like. It'll hold for 5 to 7 days in the refrigerator. I often double it and eat the leftovers on crackers, a cheese plate, or in a sandwich.

In France (and often Stateside), you can buy refrigerated sheets of all-butter puff pastry at the corner store (or supermarket), which means you're a preheated oven away from any number of flaky snacks to serve with pre-dinner drinks. Here's an especially tasty one.

In a medium saucepan over medium-high heat, add the figs and vermouth and bring to a boil. Lower the heat to medium-low and simmer until the figs are tender and the liquid has evaporated, 3 to 4 minutes.

In a food processor, combine the vermouth-plumped figs, olives, lemon zest and juice, garlic, and capers. Pulse to combine into a thick paste. With the motor running, slowly pour in the oil, processing until the mixture becomes a smooth paste. Season generously with pepper.

Preheat the oven to 400°F [200°C]. Line two baking sheets with parchment paper.

Transfer the puff pastry to a lightly floured surface and roll into a 20-by-10-inch [50 by 25 cm] rectangle (about ⅛ inch [4 mm] thick). Spread the olive tapenade on one long half of the dough rectangle, leaving a ¼-inch [6 mm] border around the edges. Fold the other half of the dough over the tapenade filling. Cut the dough crosswise into 32 strips (each about ⅔ by 5 inches [17 mm by 12 cm]).

Transfer the strips to the prepared baking sheets and, working with one strip at a time, brush lightly with the beaten egg. Twist each strip and sprinkle with black pepper. Bake until golden brown, 15 to 20 minutes. Serve warm or transfer to a cooling rack to cool completely, about 15 minutes.

GÂTEAU SALÉ (SNACK CAKE)

**Makes one
9-by-5-inch
[23 by 12 cm] cake**

5 tablespoons [75 g] unsalted European butter

1¾ cups [245 g] all-purpose flour

2 teaspoons baking powder

1 teaspoon herbes de Provence

¾ teaspoon fine sea salt

1¼ teaspoons freshly ground black pepper

⅓ cup [80 ml] whole milk

3 tablespoons grainy mustard

3 large eggs

2 cups [160 g] grated Gruyère or Emmental cheese

1 cup [160 g] mixed green and black olives, pitted and coarsely chopped

½ cup [60 g] walnuts, toasted and coarsely chopped

Savory cakes aren't something you'll find in French bakeries. They're an at-home and—for reasons I can't understand—out-of-vogue apéritif treat. It took me many years and many visits to French homes to find one in the wild, but once I did, I spent the whole apéro hour nearby. I was highly antisocial that evening, and would do it again.

Preheat the oven to 300°F [150°C]. Butter a 9-by-5-inch [23 by 12 cm] loaf pan.

In a small saucepan over medium heat, melt the butter. Cook, stirring often, until the butter is dark golden, 5 to 6 minutes, being careful not to let it burn. Scrape into a large mixing bowl and set aside to cool slightly.

In a medium bowl, whisk together the flour, baking powder, herbes de Provence, salt, and ¼ teaspoon of the pepper.

Whisk the milk and mustard into the cooled butter. Add the eggs and whisk to combine. Use a spatula to fold in the flour mixture until almost combined. Add the grated cheese, olives, and walnuts and stir just until combined.

Transfer to the prepared pan and top with the remaining 1 teaspoon of pepper. Bake until the cake is golden and set, about 45 minutes. Cool for 10 minutes in the pan before removing. Cool completely on a cooling rack or serve warm.

EGGS MAYO
WITH PERSILLADE

Serves 4 to 6

8 large eggs

¼ cup [60 g] mayonnaise (see Note, page 115)

¼ cup [60 g] Persillade (recipe follows)

1 tablespoon fresh lemon juice

Fine sea salt

Freshly ground black pepper

Flaky sea salt

Note

Eggs can be cooked and peeled up to 3 days ahead. Store in an airtight container in the refrigerator.

Eggs mayo are my apéro North Star. They're easy and delicious, and if you're running around doing a bunch of other things, your guests are fully capable of doing the heavy lifting of peeling eggs and spreading them with mayonnaise—promise! I often stir a bit of bright green, garlicky persillade into my mayo because it's pretty and easy and I love impressing people with things that actually aren't hard. Put it on my tombstone.

Fill a large bowl with ice water and set aside. Bring a large saucepan of water to a boil over medium-high heat. Using a slotted spoon, carefully lower the eggs into the water one at a time. Cook for 7 minutes, adjusting the heat as necessary to maintain a gentle boil. Transfer the eggs to the ice bath and set aside to cool.

In a medium bowl, mix together the mayonnaise, persillade, and lemon juice. Season with fine sea salt and pepper.

Use the back of a spoon to gently crack the eggs all over and peel. Halve the eggs, spread each with a bit of the mayo-persillade mixture, and arrange on a platter. Sprinkle with flaky sea salt and pepper and serve.

PERSILLADE

Makes ½ cup [120 g]

1 cup [20 g] tightly packed fresh flat-leaf parsley leaves

6 garlic cloves

½ cup [120 ml] extra-virgin olive oil

Fine sea salt

Freshly ground black pepper

In a food processor, combine the parsley, garlic, and oil. Pulse until finely chopped. Season with salt and pepper.

Note

Hate when cookbooks give you a subrecipe you use once and never again? Me too. See pages 178 and 219 for other ways to use this condiment.

Persillade is also extremely good on avocado toast, pasta, or literally anything else.

VEGETABLES WITH SAUSSOUN DIP

Serves 6

¾ cup [100 g] macadamia nuts

5 anchovy fillets

1 garlic clove, peeled

1 teaspoon fennel seeds

⅔ cup [8 g] fresh fennel fronds

⅔ cup [8 g] fresh mint leaves

½ cup [120 ml] extra-virgin olive oil

1 tablespoon fresh lemon juice

Fine sea salt

Freshly ground black pepper

Crunchy vegetables, such as radishes, carrots, celery, cucumbers, fennel, or bell peppers, sliced, for serving

Country bread, sliced and toasted, for serving

Note

Dill isn't as big of a "thing" in France, but I love it. If you do too and/or you happen to have it on hand, add in 1 or 2 tablespoons of it with the fennel fronds and mint.

In Provence, this very old, very classic dip is made with almonds, my mortal enemy. You can 100 percent sub in said almonds for the macadamia nuts used below. If you do go the macadamia route, invest in a pile and make the Macadamia Nut Brittle Ice Cream on page 259.

In a food processor, combine the macadamia nuts, anchovies, garlic, and fennel seeds and blend until finely chopped. Add the fennel fronds and mint and pulse to coarsely combine. With the mixer running, add the oil in a steady stream, blending until the sauce is smooth. Stir in the lemon juice and season with salt and pepper. Serve with crunchy vegetables and toasted bread.

PIPÉRADE DIP

Serves 6

4 medium plum tomatoes
(or one 14-ounce [400 g]
can crushed tomatoes)

3 tablespoons extra-virgin
olive oil

1 medium white onion,
thinly sliced

3 medium bell peppers
(preferably 1 green, 1 red,
and 1 yellow), seeded and
sliced into ¼-inch [6 mm]
strips

Fine sea salt

3 garlic cloves, finely
chopped

1½ teaspoons piment
d'Espelette

Crackers, bread, or crudité,
for serving

Note
Store any extra dip in the
refrigerator for a midnight
snack, to pile on toast, or to
stir into scrambled eggs in
the morning.

The red tomatoes, green bell pepper, and white onion in
pipérade represent the colors of the Basque flag. In Basque
country—located in the western Pyrenees, straddling the
border of France and Spain—you'll find pipérade served with
eggs, fish, and meat, but it's just as proud, if less traditional,
as a dip. While this recipe comes together fairly quickly, the
flavors deepen and marry with time, so if you can swing it,
make it a day or two before your apéro.

If using plum tomatoes, cut a small shallow X in the bottom of
each tomato. Prepare an ice bath in a large bowl and bring a
large pot of water to a boil. Add the tomatoes to the boiling
water and blanch until the skin starts to peel at the edges of the
cuts, 10 to 20 seconds. Drain and transfer to the ice bath. Once
the tomatoes are cooled slightly, use your fingers to peel the
skin off and discard. Roughly chop the tomatoes; set aside.

In a large skillet over medium-high heat, heat the oil until hot.
Add the onion and peppers and season with salt. Cook, stirring
often, until the onions are translucent, about 10 minutes. Add
the garlic and continue to cook for 1 minute more.

Stir in the tomatoes and piment d'Espelette, using a wooden
spoon to scrape up any bits stuck to the bottom of the pan.
Lower the heat to medium and cover the pan with a lid. Cook
until the tomatoes start to fall apart and the peppers are soft,
about 15 minutes. Remove the lid and continue to cook, stirring
frequently, until most of the liquid evaporates and the mixture
is thickened, about 10 minutes more. Season with salt and set
aside to cool slightly. Transfer to a food processor and pulse
until a slightly chunky purée forms. Serve with crackers, bread,
or crudité.

CRÈME FRAÎCHE DIP

Serves 4 to 6

6 medium shallots, thinly sliced

2 garlic cloves, finely chopped

2 tablespoons extra-virgin olive oil

4 fresh thyme sprigs, plus ½ teaspoon finely chopped thyme leaves

Fine sea salt

Freshly ground black pepper

1 tablespoon dry white wine or white wine vinegar

¾ cup [180 g] crème fraîche

¼ cup [35 g] pitted, coarsely chopped black olives

1 tablespoon fresh lemon juice

Potato chips, for serving

No one should need an excuse to keep potato chips in the house, but here's a dip, just in case.

Preheat the oven to 400°F [200°C].

On a rimmed baking sheet, toss together the shallots, garlic, oil, and thyme sprigs. Season with salt and pepper. Roast until the shallots are charred and very fragrant, 10 to 12 minutes. Remove from the oven and pour the white wine over the shallot mixture. Use a wooden spoon to scrape up any brown bits, then set aside to cool to room temperature. Remove and discard the thyme sprigs.

Scrape the shallot mixture into a medium bowl, then add the crème fraîche, olives, chopped thyme, and lemon juice. Stir to combine; season with salt and pepper. Serve with potato chips.

Note

If you know me, you know how much I appreciate an amply salted dish. That said, when serving any dip with potato chips, taste the chips before your final seasoning. Some brands are extremely well-salted, while others are less so. Tailor your dip seasoning to said dip's delivery system.

XL GOUGÈRES

Makes 12

6 tablespoons [85 g] unsalted European butter, diced

¼ cup [60 ml] whole milk

¾ teaspoon fine sea salt

½ teaspoon freshly ground black pepper, plus more for sprinkling

1¼ cups [175 g] all-purpose flour

4 large eggs, at room temperature

1½ cups [120 g] grated Gruyère, Comté, or Emmental cheese

½ cup [60 g] crumbled blue cheese

Flaky sea salt

There's a bakery down the street from my house that pulls warm, cheesy, extremely large gougères out of the oven around 9:30 a.m., so if you're ever looking for me in Paris in the morning, that's an excellent place to start.

Line two large baking sheets with parchment paper.

In a medium saucepan over medium-high heat, combine ¾ cup [180 ml] of water, the butter, milk, salt, and pepper. Heat until the butter is melted and the mixture is hot but not boiling.

Add the flour all at once, lower the heat to medium, and use a wooden spoon to stir constantly until the dough pulls away from the sides of the pan, a smooth ball forms, and the mixture starts to leave a film on the pan, 3 to 4 minutes.

Transfer the dough to the bowl of a stand mixer fitted with a paddle attachment. Mix on medium-low speed until the bowl no longer feels hot to the touch, then add the eggs, one at a time, making sure each is mixed in before adding the next. Once all the eggs are added, increase the speed to medium-high and beat for 15 minutes. Add 1¼ cups [100 g] of the Gruyère and the blue cheese and mix just to combine.

Use a large ice cream scoop to mound the dough into twelve 2½- to 3-inch [6 to 7.5 cm] rounds on one of the prepared baking sheets. Freeze the gougères for at least 1 hour (or in an airtight container for up to 1 month).

Preheat the oven to 400°F [200°C].

Transfer six of the gougère mounds to the second baking sheet, arranging them about 2 inches [5 cm] apart. Arrange the remaining six gougères, replacing the parchment paper if needed. Sprinkle with the remaining ¼ cup [20 g] of Gruyère cheese, more pepper, and flaky salt.

Bake for 15 minutes, then lower the oven temperature to 375°F [190°C] and continue to bake, rotating the pans halfway through, until the gougères are puffed and deeply golden brown, 20 to 30 minutes more. Serve warm. Gougères are best the day they are baked.

BAKED CAMEMBERT

Serves 4 to 6

One 4- to 5-inch [10 to
12 cm] wheel Camembert,
cut into 1-inch [2.5 cm]
pieces

8 pitted dates, torn into
pieces

1 teaspoon fresh thyme
leaves

Piment d'Espelette Oil
(page 86) or chile oil, for
drizzling

Crackers or crusty bread,
for serving

It's nothing new, but baked cheese is damn delicious. Instead
of throwing a whole wheel in the oven and calling it a life, I cut
the wheel into pieces in order to ensure that there are plenty
of dates throughout (unlike in my life, heyo!). The flavors here
veer outside the ordinary wheelhouse of hot fromage: funky
Camembert, sweet dried fruit, earthy thyme, and to finish, a
spiced oil that feels a little reckless over a soft, French cheese,
but in a good way, obviously.

Preheat the oven to 350°F [180°C].

Tuck the Camembert pieces into a 4- to 5-inch [10 to 12 cm]
ovenproof baking dish and add the dates in the spaces between
the cheese. Sprinkle with thyme and bake until the cheese is
bubbling, 25 to 30 minutes. Drizzle with the piment d'Espelette
oil and serve with crackers or crusty bread.

UPGRADED POTATO CHIPS

Serves 6 to 8

1 tablespoon smoked paprika

1 teaspoon sugar

½ teaspoon ground cumin

¼ teaspoon freshly ground black pepper

¼ teaspoon fine sea salt, plus more as needed

Generous pinch of cayenne pepper

Two 5-ounce [140 g] bags kettle-cooked salted potato chips

In even the tiniest of supermarchés, the French keep their potato chip aisle extremely well stocked. Salty, communal, and perfect between sips, a bag is the ideal apéritif snack to pick up on the way to the Seine or the park or your couch. This recipe elevates that quick grab without much additional effort. Start with a spice combination that calls to mind barbecue chips of your youth, then play with whatever flavor profile you're feeling that night. Serve in a bowl, or do as I do and return the updated chips, adorably, to their conveniently portable bag and serve alongside the first drink of the night.

Preheat the oven to 300°F [150°C].

In a small bowl, mix together the paprika, sugar, cumin, black pepper, salt, and cayenne.

On a rimmed baking sheet, spread the potato chips out in a single layer. Bake until warmed through, about 5 minutes.

Transfer the warm potato chips to a large bowl. While the chips are still warm, sprinkle them with the spice mixture and toss gently to coat. Taste and season with more salt if needed. Serve warm or at room temperature.

SOCCA + PARM

Makes 2 pancakes / Serves 6 to 8

1 cup [100 g] fine chickpea flour

4 tablespoons [60 ml] extra-virgin olive oil

¾ teaspoon fine sea salt

½ teaspoon freshly ground black pepper

¼ teaspoon piment d'Espelette, plus more to finish

Piment d'Espelette Oil (recipe follows)

Flaky sea salt

Wedge of Parmesan, crumbled into bite-size pieces, for serving

One of the best (read: easiest) things to put out for guests is a big piece of Parmesan with a knife, crackers, and a pinch of red pepper flakes. The combination of pantry essentials provides the perfect salt-and-spice crossover to snack on during apéro hour. This recipe takes that general idea, tapping in socca and a quickly made piment d'Espelette oil. The batter for the socca—essentially a large chickpea pancake from Provence served warm and roughly cut—can and should be made in advance and broiled when your first guest is crossing the threshold.

In a medium bowl, whisk together the chickpea flour, 1 cup [240 ml] of lukewarm water, 2 tablespoons of the olive oil, the fine sea salt, pepper, and piment d'Espelette. Cover and let sit at room temperature for at least 2 hours and up to overnight.

Preheat the broiler and arrange an oven rack near the top of the oven. Add 1 tablespoon of the olive oil to a 10-inch [25 cm] cast-iron skillet and place it in the oven until hot, about 10 minutes. Carefully remove the pan from the oven and pour in half the batter. Gently swirl the pan to coat, then return to the oven and broil until the socca is golden brown and starting to char in spots, 2 to 3 minutes. Transfer to a plate and drizzle with piment d'Espelette oil and sprinkle with flaky salt. Repeat with the remaining 1 tablespoon of olive oil and the socca batter. Serve the crumbled Parmesan alongside.

PIMENT D'ESPELETTE OIL

Makes ½ cup [120 ml]

½ cup [120 ml] extra-virgin olive oil

1 teaspoon piment d'Espelette

Warming the oil slightly allows the piment d'Espelette to infuse, but be sure to keep it from getting too hot—it'll burn the delicate spice.

In a small saucepan over medium-low heat, heat the oil until just warmed. Remove the pan from the heat, add the piment d'Espelette, and stir to combine. Set aside to cool and infuse. The oil will keep at room temperature in a tightly sealed container for 1 month.

SARDINE RILLETTES

Serves 6

Two 5-ounce [140 g] tins sardines packed in oil

½ lemon, zested and juiced

6 tablespoons [85 g] salted European butter, at room temperature (see Note)

Freshly ground black pepper

Crusty bread, for serving

Note
If you don't have salted butter on hand—or it's very lightly salted—season with fine or flaky sea salt.

À Table wouldn't be a French cookbook without some form of rillettes. These are the simplest—but no less delicious—of them all, requiring only two motor skills: opening a can of good sardines and smashing things together with a fork.

Drain the sardines from their oil, reserving the oil for another use. In a medium bowl, add the sardines and lemon zest and use a fork to crush the sardines into small pieces. Add the lemon juice, butter, and pepper and use the fork to mix together until combined. Season with more pepper if desired and serve with bread.

SHRIMP COCKTAIL, BUT MAKE IT FRENCH

Serves 6 to 8

Shrimp

2 lemons

2 tablespoons fine sea salt

1 bay leaf

1½ pounds [680 g] large shrimp (24 to 30 shrimp), peeled and deveined

Rémoulade

1 cup [240 g] mayonnaise (see Note, page 115)

1 tablespoon fresh lemon juice

2 teaspoons Dijon mustard

1 anchovy fillet, finely chopped

¼ cup [40 g] finely chopped cornichons

2 tablespoons finely chopped fresh flat-leaf parsley

1 tablespoon finely chopped fresh chives

1 tablespoon finely chopped fresh chervil (optional)

1½ teaspoons salted capers, rinsed, drained, and finely chopped

Note

The rémoulade can be made up to 2 days in advance (and the flavors get even better, so if you're patient or have leftovers, you're in for a real treat).

Classic French rémoulade is basically Thousand Island dressing meets tartar sauce, and I love this meeting. This recipe is best experienced alongside a few 50/50s (page 45), but I'm not going to force you to enjoy the best pairing of your life.

Prepare an ice bath in a large bowl and set aside.

To make the shrimp: Fill a large pot with water and set it over high heat. Cut the lemons in half and squeeze into the pot; add the lemon halves, salt, and bay leaf and bring to a boil. Stir to dissolve the salt, then let boil for 10 minutes.

To make the rémoulade: In a medium bowl, stir together the mayonnaise, lemon juice, mustard, and anchovy. Add the cornichons, parsley, chives, chervil (if using), and capers. Stir to combine.

Remove the poaching liquid from the heat and add the shrimp. Poach until the shrimp begin to curl and turn pink, 3 to 3½ minutes. Use a slotted spoon to transfer the shrimp to the prepared ice bath and chill for 3 to 5 minutes, then drain the shrimp well and serve with the rémoulade.

OYSTERS ON THE ROCKS

Serves as many people as you have

Classic Mignonette

¼ cup [60 ml] red wine vinegar

¼ cup [35 g] finely chopped shallots

1 teaspoon freshly ground black pepper

Pinch of sugar

Muscadet-Fennel Mignonette

2 tablespoons Muscadet wine or other dry white wine

2 tablespoons white wine vinegar

¼ cup [10 g] finely chopped fennel fronds

½ teaspoon ground white pepper

4 or 5 oysters per person, shucked just before serving

Lemon wedges, for serving

Note

Every time I've eaten oysters in France, they come with sliced bread and (very good) salted butter. Not exactly a mandate, but if you're feeling traditional, I highly recommend.

Crushed ice cubes are your rocks here. To crush, double up two large freezer bags, fill halfway with ice, and seal. Then take a rolling pin or cast-iron skillet or whatever other hard, heavy object you have nearby, and smash on a stable surface (say, the floor) until the ice is the size of beans. Transfer to a shallow serving plate, platter, or quarter baking sheet and freeze for 30 minutes before nestling in freshly shucked oysters and little bowls of mignonette.

To make the Classic Mignonette: In a small bowl, combine the red wine vinegar, shallots, black pepper, and sugar. Stir to combine and let sit for at least 10 minutes.

To make the Muscadet-Fennel Mignonette: In another small bowl, combine the wine, vinegar, fennel fronds, and white pepper.

Fill a serving dish with crushed ice. Scrub the oysters well under cold running water, checking for and discarding any opened shells.

Place an oyster, round-side down, in a folded kitchen towel so the hinge is exposed. Steady the oyster with the palm of your hand, bunching up the towel around your hand. Wiggle the oyster knife into the hinge, working the knife up and down and twisting gently until you feel the seal pop. Separate the top shell from the bottom, clean the knife, then work around the perimeter of the shell to sever the muscle that attaches the top of the shell to the meat. Discard the top shell. Wipe your knife clean again, then sever the muscle from the bottom shell. Repeat until all the oysters are shucked. Serve with the mignonettes and lemon wedges.

WHOLE ARTICHOKES WITH BUTTER + ZA'ATAR

Serves 6

Artichokes

3 large artichokes

½ lemon, thinly sliced

2 garlic cloves, smashed

1 teaspoon whole black peppercorns

Dipping Sauce

½ cup [110 g] unsalted European butter

1 garlic clove, finely grated on a Microplane

1 teaspoon Dijon mustard

½ teaspoon freshly ground black pepper

3 tablespoons za'atar

1 teaspoon flaky sea salt

Honestly, just thinking about preparing artichokes tires me out. More often, I opt for a high-quality jar of artichoke hearts, to excellent results. But there's really nothing like ripping apart the whole thing in a messy excuse to consume copious amounts of butter. To do that, you need to "prepare them" for steaming. That said, below is a recipe that employs the easiest preparation out there: tricking your guests into de-choking them themselves once they near that harshly protected tender heart. The whole affair is *almost* as easy as opening a jar.

To prepare the artichokes: Use a bread knife to cut off the top quarter of each artichoke as well as the stems (this will help the artichokes stand upright). Pull off the tough bottom leaves, then use a pair of scissors to cut away the thorny ends of each of the remaining leaves.

In a large steamer or pot over high heat, add enough water to come 2 inches [5 cm] up the side of the pot. Bring to a boil. Add the lemon slices, garlic cloves, peppercorns, and artichokes, stem-side down, to the steamer basket or directly in the water. Turn the heat to low, cover the pot, and simmer until the leaves easily pull away and a paring knife inserted in the center of the artichokes slips through without any resistance, 45 minutes to 1 hour.

While the artichokes cook, make the dipping sauce: In a small saucepan over medium heat, melt the butter. Whisk in the grated garlic and cook for 30 seconds. Remove the pan from the heat and whisk in the mustard and pepper. Pour into a small dish for serving.

In another small dish, combine the za'atar and flaky salt. Serve the artichokes hot or at room temperature with the garlic butter and za'atar salt for sprinkling.

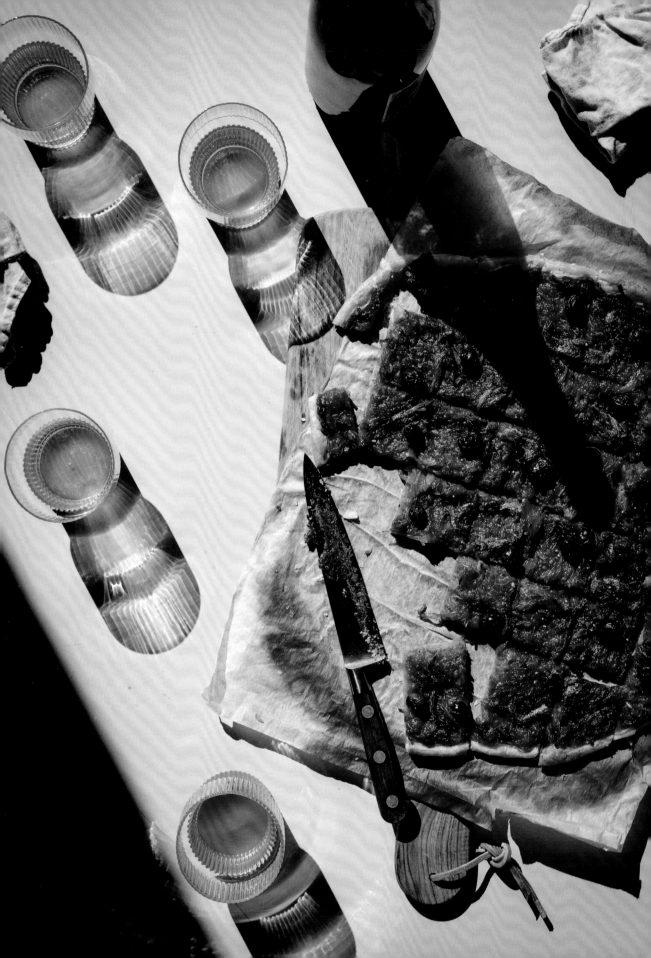

PICHADE DE MENTON

Serves 6 to 8

4 medium plum tomatoes
(or one 14-ounce [400 g]
can crushed tomatoes)

¼ cup [60 ml] extra-virgin
olive oil

3 pounds [1.4 kg] white
onions, thinly sliced

18 anchovies packed in
olive oil

2 fresh thyme sprigs

One 14-ounce [400 g]
package all-butter puff
pastry

⅓ cup [55 g] Niçoise olives

Note

If you want to make a
pissaladière, scrap the
tomatoes entirely and add
the thyme to the onions right
at the start.

Traditionally the base is made
with yeasted dough, but you
can also make it with store-
bought all-butter puff pastry.
I'm a fan of the latter because
I'm saving my dough making
for another hard-to-pronounce
but fun-to-eat French recipe:
the Kouign-Amann (page 252).

I'm pretty sure my editors wanted me to translate this recipe
title to something non–French speakers can pronounce, but
translations can get complicated . . . and boring. Pichade de
Menton is a pissaladière with tomatoes added. A pissaladière
is, roughly, an onion tart with anchovies and olives, so you
could say a pichade de Menton is a tomato-onion tart with
anchovies and olives. I don't know about you, but even in my
terrible French accent, I much prefer the très chic "pichade de
Menton," but you do you.

If using plum tomatoes, cut a small shallow *X* in the bottom of
each tomato. Prepare an ice bath in a large bowl and bring a
large pot of water to a boil. Add the tomatoes to the boiling
water and blanch until the skin starts to peel at the edges of the
cuts, 10 to 20 seconds. Drain and transfer to the ice bath. Once
the tomatoes are cooled slightly, use your fingers to peel the
skin off and discard. Roughly chop the tomatoes; set aside.

In a large skillet over medium heat, add the olive oil and onions.
Cover the pan and cook, stirring occasionally, until the onions
are soft, about 30 minutes. Uncover and continue to cook,
stirring occasionally, until the liquid evaporates and the onions
are very golden brown, 30 to 45 minutes more. Finely chop four
of the anchovies and add them to the onion mixture. Cook for
30 seconds, then add the tomatoes and thyme and continue to
cook until the liquid fully evaporates, about 20 minutes. Remove
the thyme sprigs.

Preheat the oven to 400°F [200°C]. Line a baking sheet with
parchment paper.

Unfold the puff pastry onto the prepared baking sheet and
use a fork to prick the pastry all over. Spread the onion-tomato
mixture in an even layer over the puff pastry, leaving a ¼-inch
[6 mm] border around the edges. Top with the remaining
fourteen whole anchovies. Scatter the olives evenly over the
top and bake the pastry until the edges and bottom are golden
brown, 20 to 25 minutes. Cut into pieces and serve warm or at
room temperature.

LE GRAND AÏOLI II

Serves 6 to 8

2 large egg yolks

1 teaspoon Dijon mustard

1 garlic clove, grated

½ cup [120 ml] grapeseed or canola oil

¼ cup [60 ml] extra-virgin olive oil

1 lemon, juiced

Fine sea salt

Freshly ground black pepper

Boiled or steamed vegetables, such as small potatoes, cauliflower, broccoli, haricots verts, and/or asparagus, for serving

Raw vegetables and greens, such as celery, bell peppers, fennel, endive, quartered small heads of lettuce, radishes, cucumbers, cherry tomatoes, and/or carrots, for serving

4 large soft-boiled eggs, peeled and halved, for serving

1 or 2 tins sardines packed in oil, for serving

Note
I have these ridiculously delicious yuzu sesame seeds I picked up at a Japanese market in the 2ème that I tend to sprinkle on tinned fish to excellent result. Do that if you like, don't if you don't.

Often when people find out I live in Paris, they assume I knew French before moving or, at the very least, know it now. I'm always sad to correct them, but I studied Spanish in high school, German in college, and while I know more now than I did when I first moved—nada, nichts, rien—French is an ongoing battle. I do imagine, however, that le grand aïoli is the recipe equivalent of French fluency. It requires less thought than instinct to arrange colorful vegetables around the garlic-laced aïoli, and the resulting vibe of your apéro is relaxed, secure in the foundation of a solid, interactive snack. Oftentimes le grand aïoli, a Provençal classic, is served with fish or roasted chicken to make it a meal. Here, tinned fish subs in to keep it uncomplicated and versatile.

In a medium bowl, whisk together the yolks, mustard, and garlic. Whisking constantly, add the grapeseed oil drop by drop until the mixture thickens. Continuing to whisk constantly, pour in the remainder of the grapeseed oil and the olive oil in a slow, steady stream. Add the lemon juice in 1-teaspoon increments, whisking constantly. The aïoli mixture should be pale yellow and thick. Season with salt and pepper and transfer to a serving bowl.

Arrange the vegetables, greens, eggs, sardines, and bowl of aïoli on a platter and serve.

À TABLE

YOUR DEFINITIVE GUIDE TO MEAT ON A BOARD, PLATE, OR SLATE

Good charcuterie is one of the cornerstones of French food culture. You have your saucisson, your jamon de Bayonne, your pâté. Skip across one of France's many borders to Spain, Italy, Switzerland, or Germany, and the options continue to grow. Do as the French do and be generous in portion size and ruthless with quality control.

Here's how: Go to your butcher, taste a bunch of things, choose the one that's the most delicious. A hill on which I will die: It is far better to have one great type of charcuterie (and lots of it) rather than a muddled collection of too-small or too-few meats. Choose the one you love and then think about the bread or cracker just for it, the pickle or mustard just for it. You can keep your five meats fanned out on a board; give me a thick slice of country pâté, a generous handful of cornichons, and a knife.

One exception to this one-meat rule: If your idea of the most delicious charcuterie is blood sausage, by all means, but also get something for the less intrepid but no less cured meat–loving among us.

Here's a short guide to some French and French-adjacent favorites in my house. Use it as you like, but also trust your taste buds and your butcher.

JAMBON DE BAYONNE—*French*

Often referred to as the Champagne of ham, and just like Champagne can only be from Champagne, jambon de Bayonne can only be from the Bayonne region in the southwest of France. It's salted and air-dried, slightly sweet, not overly salty, and generally sliced paper-thin. If you can't find it, go for Italy's prosciutto or Spain's Jamón Serrano.

COPPA—*Italian*

Also called capicola or capocollo, coppa is smooth in texture with a strong, fatty, well-seasoned flavor. It comes in both hot and sweet and, depending on where in Italy your coppa is from, has a range of different seasonings.

SAUCISSON SEC—*French*

Thick, dry-cured, and generally pork sausage, saucisson sec is similar to Italy's dry-cured salamis or my Wisco motherland's summer sausage. It's salty and savory and comes in varieties containing cheese, truffles, dried fruits, or nuts.

VIANDE DES GRISONS—*Swiss*

This thinly sliced, salted, air-dried beef is also called Bündnerfleisch in German. It can be hard to find in the United States, so go for the Italian version: bresaola.

SOPPRESSATA—*Italian*

This hard salami from southern Italy is a safe but very good bet (when done well) for a mixed crowd.

FINOCCHIONA—*Italian*

Dry-cured and made from pork shoulder and cheek with fennel, black pepper, and garlic, it's the closest I can get to having a godmother sandwich on the beach in LA without being within driving distance of Bay Cities Italian Deli. Just me?

MORTADELLA—*Italian*

An emulsified pork sausage (read: bologna) with spices, fatback, and often pistachios, mortadella has a smooth, nearly creamy texture and hammy flavor. I crave mortadella once a year and every year it's perfect.

PÂTÉ, TERRINES, RILLETTES—*French*

Pâtés, terrines, and rillettes are all considered part of the charcuterie family in France and often set out before a meal alongside a bit of bread and not much else. I'm partial to pâté de campagne, a common, rustic pâté in loaf form, often bolstered by onions, pepper, and cognac.

À TABLE

*REMARQUE
ON SNACK DINNER

When I first started gathering people chez moi, I found the most accessible,
low-stress, high-quality entry point to having people over during what
should be dinnertime is throwing an apéro dînatoire—also called apéritif
dînatoire. Not quite drinks and dash, not quite coursed sit-down dinner,
France's apéro dînatoire is the happy love child of the two. Mainly, it's a
chic way to eat snacks for dinner, and let's be honest, sometimes snack
dinner is way more fun than dinner dinner. To throw your own, choose a few
drinks and snacks from the Before section of this book (page 29). Alternate
between favorites or throw darts; they all work. You could also sneak into
the other sections of the book and add in, say, a Tomato Tart (page 166) or
Carrot Tarte Tatin (page 223) as long as you cut them into snackable pieces.
Hell, also drop into the Digestifs section (page 274) as the night wears on.
Basically, apéro dînatoire offers you carte blanche to serve whatever you
like as long as it's simple and abundant and promotes continuous eating
with one hand while the other holds a drink.

DURING

SUPPER + SIDES

DURING

Mains

---

*REMARQUE

Sides

Carrots with Piment d'Espelette 186

Parsnips with Fennel +
Honeycomb 189

Roasted Nectarines + Shallots 190

Haricots Verts with Tapenade 192

Tomates Oubliées 193

Tomatoes with Butter +
Armagnac 195

Eggplant Confit 196

Roasted Yellow Peppers with
Cornichons + Capers 199

(Roasted) Radishes with Butter 200

Légumes Farcis 202

Red Kuri Squash with Cider +
Saucisson 205

Lazy Dux 206

Greens with Roasted Tomato
Vinaigrette 207

Sucrine Wedge 208

Salade Verte with Cornichon
Vinaigrette 210

Parsley Salad 211

Escarole Salad with Concord Grapes 212

Extremely French Carrot Salad 215

Caramelized Endive Salad 216

Lentil Salad with Persillade 219

Buttered Peas + Greens 220

Carrot Tarte Tatin 223

Frites 224

Potatoes, Artichokes + Shallots 226

Pommes Anna 227

Gratin Dauphinois (a.k.a. French
Scalloped Potatoes) 229

Aligot (Mashed Potatoes
with Cheese) 230

Beans with Pistachio Aïllade 231

Beans Longtemps 232

MAINS

COQ AU VERMOUTH

Serves 6

3 pounds [1.4 kg] chicken legs and thighs

Fine sea salt

Ground white pepper

4 ounces [115 g] lardons or bacon, cut crosswise into ¼-inch [6 mm] strips

1 medium yellow onion, quartered and thinly sliced

4 medium carrots, cut into 1- to 1½-inch [2.5 to 4 cm] diagonal slices

4 garlic cloves, finely chopped

8 ounces [230 g] cremini mushrooms, quartered

2 fresh thyme sprigs

1½ cups [360 ml] dry vermouth

2 tablespoons unsalted European butter

1 to 2 tablespoons fresh lemon juice

Note

Using only bone-in dark meat instead of the classic whole chicken cut into pieces makes the final dish richer and thicker and less likely to contain any dry meat. If you do prefer to use a whole chicken cut into pieces, add the breasts to the pot about 10 minutes after adding the dark meat.

There's a reason I put this recipe on the cover. It's everything I (and hopefully you, dear reader) want in a chicken dish: extra-tender meat, ample vegetables, and a rich, deeply aromatic sauce abundant enough to serve with as much crusty bread as the heart desires. The keys to the layers of flavor are to brown the lardons extremely well in the beginning, season generously and often, and invest in a dry vermouth you would drink on its own over ice or in a cocktail.

Season the chicken with salt and white pepper.

In a large Dutch oven or pot over medium heat, add the lardons and cook, stirring occasionally, until very well browned and crisp, 5 to 7 minutes. Use a slotted spoon to transfer the lardons to a plate. Add the chicken pieces in a single layer to the pot, working in batches as needed, and cook until well browned on both sides, about 5 minutes on each side. Transfer to the platter with the lardons.

Add the onion and carrots to the pot and cook, stirring occasionally, until golden brown and the carrots start to soften, about 10 minutes. Stir in the garlic, mushrooms, and thyme sprigs; season with salt. Cook for 5 minutes, then pour in the vermouth and increase the heat to medium-high. Return the chicken (see Note) and lardons as well as any juices on the plate to the pot, nestling them into the vegetable mixture. Bring to a simmer, then lower the heat to maintain a gentle simmer. Cover the pot and cook, basting occasionally, until the chicken is very tender and cooked through, about 30 minutes.

Remove the lid, transfer the chicken to a platter, and increase the heat to medium-high. Cook until the sauce thickens slightly, about 5 minutes, then stir in the butter and lemon juice. Once the butter is melted, return the chicken to the pot for a few minutes to rewarm. Season with salt and white pepper as needed. Serve warm.

ROAST CHICKEN WITH PRUNES

Serves 6

One 3- to 4-pound [1.4 to 1.8 kg] chicken

Fine sea salt

Freshly ground black pepper

1 head garlic, halved crosswise

1 lemon, halved crosswise

1½ pounds [680 g] very small waxy potatoes

1 cup [180 g] prunes (15 to 18), pitted

¼ cup [30 g] salted capers, soaked, rinsed, and drained

4 tablespoons [60 ml] extra-virgin olive oil

2 tablespoons red wine vinegar

1 bay leaf

One of my favorite holidays to spend in France is Thanksgiving. One, because Thanksgiving in America needs a big decolonization, and two, because introducing the French people in my life to the glory that is pecan pie is the gift that keeps on giving. This recipe comes straight from one of those late November dinners. Since turkey isn't common in France, we did what folks should maybe do for Thanksgiving anyway and roasted a chicken instead. The real star of the dish, however, are the prunes: They become plump and rich and soften to an almost cranberry sauce–like texture.

Preheat the oven to 300°F [150°C].

Pat the chicken dry with paper towels and season inside and out with salt and pepper. Place one of the garlic head halves and one lemon half in the cavity of the chicken. Tie the legs together with kitchen twine.

Arrange the potatoes, prunes, and capers in a Dutch oven or large cast-iron skillet; drizzle with 2 tablespoons of the oil and the vinegar. Season with salt and pepper. Toss to coat, then make a space in the center big enough for the chicken. Add the remaining garlic half (cut-side down) and the bay leaf in the center of the skillet, then place the chicken, breast-side up, on top. Drizzle the chicken with the remaining 2 tablespoons of oil.

Roast until the potatoes are very tender and the chicken is deep golden brown, 2½ to 3 hours. Transfer the chicken to a cutting board and set aside to rest for 15 minutes. Squeeze the juice from the second lemon half over the potato-prune mixture and toss to coat. Season with salt and pepper. Serve warm.

Caramelized Endive Salad | page 216

MAYO ROAST CHICKEN

Serves 4

One 4- to 5-pound
[1.8 to 2.3 kg] chicken,
spatchcocked (see Note)

Fine sea salt

Freshly ground black
pepper

1 cup [240 g] mayonnaise
(see Note)

2 garlic cloves, grated

1 lemon, zested

1 teaspoon Dijon mustard

1 tablespoon fresh lemon
juice

2 tablespoons finely
chopped fresh chives

1 to 2 teaspoons smoked
paprika

Note
The term "spatchcocking" not
only rolls off the tongue nicely
but also describes a method
of splitting a chicken to speed
up the cooking process. To
spatchcock, take a pair of
sharp kitchen shears (or a very
sharp knife) and cut along
both sides of the chicken's
backbone. Remove it (save for
stock!), open up the bird so
it lies flat, and roast breast-
side up.

Whenever I have a dinner party planned but also a day or week full of modern-life nonsense, I stop at my rotisserie shop for a perfectly roasted chicken. I transfer from paper bag to platter to table, adding a generous side of doctored mayonnaise and a green salad.

This recipe is *almost* as simple as the semi-homemade version and leans just as hard on the mayo assist. Season the store-bought mayo with garlic, lemon, and mustard (or make your own! See Note). Rub half the mixture all over the bird and save the rest to serve alongside. During roasting, the mayonnaise plays a dual role by helping keep the meat tender and rendering the skin crisp. Honestly, do this once a week and be happy with your choices.

Preheat the oven to 450°F [230°C].

Place the chicken, breast-side up, on a rimmed baking sheet and pat dry with paper towels. Season all over with salt and pepper and set aside for 30 minutes at room temperature.

In a small bowl, stir together the mayonnaise, garlic, lemon zest, and mustard. Rub the chicken all over with ½ cup [120 g] of the mayonnaise mixture, reserving the rest. Season with salt and pepper. Roast until cooked through, 35 to 40 minutes. Let the chicken rest for 10 minutes before serving.

Meanwhile, stir the lemon juice, chives, and paprika into the reserved mayonnaise mixture. Season with salt and pepper. Transfer the chicken to a serving platter and serve the mayonnaise alongside.

Note
To make homemade mayon-
naise, in a medium bowl, whisk
together 2 large egg yolks and
1 teaspoon of Dijon mustard.
Whisking constantly, *as slowly
and gradually as possible—*
literally drop by drop—add
some of ½ cup [120 ml] of
grapeseed oil until the mixture
thickens. Continuing to whisk
constantly, start to slowly pour
in the remainder of the grapeseed oil and ¼ cup [60 ml]
of olive oil in a slow, steady
stream. Just as slowly, whisk
in 2 teaspoons of lemon juice
and season with salt and
pepper.

Parsley Salad | page 211

BASQUE CHICKEN

Serves 4 to 6

6 medium plum tomatoes (or one 28-ounce [800 g] can crushed tomatoes)

One 4- to 5-pound [1.8 to 2.3 kg] chicken, cut into eight pieces

Fine sea salt

4 tablespoons [60 ml] extra-virgin olive oil

3 ounces [85 g] Bayonne ham or prosciutto, diced

2 garlic cloves, finely chopped

2 medium yellow onions, thinly sliced

2 medium red bell peppers, sliced into ¼-inch [6 mm] strips

2 medium green bell peppers, sliced into ¼-inch [6 mm] strips

½ cup [120 ml] dry white or rosé wine

2 fresh thyme sprigs

1 bay leaf

1½ teaspoons piment d'Espelette

Basque chicken is from exactly where it advertises to be from. Basque country is one of the most spectacular and dramatic regions in France (and Spain), and the food is as vibrant as the landscape. This classic dish is deeply flavored and just on the right side of spiced, care of the region's famed chile, piment d'Espelette. Use Bayonne ham (also from Basque country!) if you can find it, prosciutto if you can't. I make mine with rosé, which isn't traditional but is delicious and leaves no question as to which wine to serve alongside.

If using plum tomatoes, cut a small shallow X in the bottom of each tomato. Prepare an ice bath in a large bowl and bring a large pot of water to a boil. Add the tomatoes to the boiling water and blanch until the skin starts to peel at the edges of the cuts, 10 to 20 seconds. Drain and transfer to the ice bath. Once the tomatoes are cooled slightly, use your fingers to peel off the skin and discard. Roughly chop the tomatoes; set aside.

Season the chicken pieces with salt. In a Dutch oven or large pot over medium heat, add 3 tablespoons of the oil. Add the chicken to the pan, skin-side down (working in batches, if needed). Cook until the skin is golden brown, 8 to 10 minutes, then transfer the chicken to a plate and set aside. Add the ham to the pot and cook, stirring occasionally, until browned and crisp, about 6 minutes. Transfer the ham to the plate with the chicken.

Add the remaining 1 tablespoon of oil to the pot and add the garlic and onions. Cook, stirring occasionally, until the onions are soft and starting to brown, about 8 minutes. Add the bell peppers and season with salt. Continue to cook, stirring occasionally, until the peppers start to soften, 8 to 10 minutes. Add the wine, reserved chopped tomatoes, the thyme, bay leaf, and piment d'Espelette and lower the heat to a simmer. Return the chicken and ham to the pot and cover, leaving the lid slightly ajar. Cook for 20 minutes.

Remove the lid and continue cooking until the liquid is almost completely reduced, 30 to 40 minutes more. Season with salt and serve warm.

CHICKEN CONFIT

Serves 6

4 pounds [1.8 kg] skin-on, bone-in chicken thighs (6 to 8)

1½ tablespoons fine sea salt, plus more as needed

1 teaspoon freshly ground black pepper, plus more as needed

1 lemon, thinly sliced

4 garlic cloves, smashed, plus 2 garlic heads, unpeeled and halved crosswise

4 fresh thyme sprigs

2 bay leaves

2 large leeks, tough outer layer and dark tops removed, halved, cleaned, and cut into 1-inch [2.5 cm] pieces

5 to 6 cups [1.2 to 1.4 L] extra-virgin olive oil

1½ cups [240 g] green olives, such as Picholine or Lucques

There's a lot of chicken in this book and I'm fine with it. (Well, I wrote it, so I hope *you're* fine with it, ma chère.) Originally, I had thought to include a recipe for duck confit because France, but let's be perfectly honest—duck confit is a once-a-year dish for the same season as raclette (page 171), and raclette wins (did I mention it's on page 171?). Chicken confit, however, is a meal I make just as often in swimsuit weather as I do the dark gray of winter. Also, it's way more affordable, and when you're cooking for a crowd on a regular basis, that matters. One thing: This recipe is incredibly simple to make, but you do need to season the chicken the night before, so plan accordingly.

Pat the chicken dry with paper towels and season with the salt and pepper. Transfer to a bowl along with the lemon slices, garlic cloves, thyme, and bay leaves and cover with a lid or an upside-down dinner plate. Refrigerate overnight.

Preheat the oven to 275°F [135°C].

Place the leeks and garlic head halves in the bottom of a large Dutch oven. Add the chicken, lemon slices, and herbs. Pour in the oil (it should cover the chicken completely) and cover the pot with a tight-fitting lid. Bake for 2 hours, then add the olives to the pot and return to the oven for 15 minutes more.

Preheat the broiler. Set an ovenproof cooling rack on a baking sheet and use a slotted spoon to transfer the chicken thighs to the rack. Broil until the chicken skin is crisp and browned, 5 to 8 minutes depending on the strength of your broiler.

Transfer the chicken thighs to a serving platter and use the slotted spoon to fish out the leeks, olives, garlic, and lemons and scatter them around the chicken. Serve warm.

(Roasted) Radishes with Butter | page 200

PARTY STEAK

Serves 6 to 8

One 3- to 4-pound [1.4 to 1.8 kg] or two 1½- to 2-pound [680 to 910 g] bone-in rib-eye or strip loin steaks, about 1½ inches [4 cm] thick (see Note)

Fine sea salt

Freshly ground black pepper

½ cup [110 g] unsalted European butter

4 garlic cloves, finely chopped

3 roasted red bell peppers, sliced (see Note, page 153)

2 large bunches fresh flat-leaf parsley, leaves picked and coarsely chopped

¼ cup [60 ml] red wine vinegar

2 tablespoons vegetable oil

Flaky sea salt

Note

I know it's sometimes hard to find a steak big enough both in form and budget, so just use as many steaks as you need to get up to 3 to 4 pounds [1.4 to 1.8 kg] of meat. Because here's the thing: The party—as all good parties are—is more a result of what happens around the edible reason we came to the table. In the case of Party Steak, it's the combination of butter, garlic, roasted red peppers, and herbs that mingle with the resting steak's juices and become a saucy, addictive, fête-worthy accompaniment.

Serve Party Steak with Frites (page 224) to people who define *party* the same way you do . . . for me, that means an early start time and lots of natural wine.

Pat the steaks dry with paper towels and season generously with fine sea salt and pepper. Set aside at room temperature for 30 minutes to 1 hour.

In a small saucepan over medium heat, combine the butter and garlic. Heat until the butter melts and the garlic begins to toast, about 2 minutes, then remove from the heat and stir in the roasted bell peppers, parsley, and vinegar. Season with fine sea salt and pepper; transfer to a serving platter.

Set a large cast-iron skillet or grill pan over medium-high heat. Once the pan is hot, add the vegetable oil and swirl to coat. Add the steaks, pressing gently to make sure the entire surface is touching the pan (work in batches if necessary). Cook until a golden brown crust has formed, 4 to 5 minutes; flip the steaks and continue to cook until browned on the second side and medium-rare (an instant-read thermometer inserted into the thickest part should register 120°F [50°C]), about 4 minutes more.

Place the steak on top of the butter-pepper mixture on the serving platter and set aside to rest for 10 minutes. Move the steak to a cutting board and slice against the grain into ½-inch [12 mm] slices. Return the slices to the platter along with any of the juices from the cutting board, sprinkle with flaky salt, and serve.

Frites | page 224

DAUBE DE BOEUF

Serves 6

3½ pounds [1.6 kg]
boneless beef chuck,
trimmed and cut into 2-inch
[5 cm] pieces

Fine sea salt

Freshly ground black
pepper

6 tablespoons [90 ml]
extra-virgin olive oil

One 750 ml bottle dry red
wine

¼ cup [60 ml] cognac,
bourbon, brandy, or
Armagnac

6 fresh thyme sprigs

2 bay leaves

4 ounces [115 g] pancetta
or bacon, cut into ¼-inch
[6 mm] pieces

2 medium yellow onions,
quartered and thinly sliced

4 garlic cloves, smashed

4 medium carrots, cut into
1½-inch [4 cm] diagonal
slices

⅓ cup [75 g] tomato paste

1 pound [455 g] small
whole-wheat pasta such as
trofie or fusilli

2 tablespoons unsalted
European butter

¼ cup [10 g] finely chopped
fresh flat-leaf parsley

You know what I thought I had when creating this recipe . . .
more than once? Brandy. So bourbon subbed in one time and
cognac another and now I make it with whatever brown-ish
spirit happens to be in the house. Speaking of swaps, if you
don't have a daubière (who does?), use a Dutch oven or a
large heavy pot and place a circle of parchment paper directly
on top of the stew; it will simulate a real daubière by limiting
evaporation and make for a richer final dish.

In a large bowl, add the beef and season with salt and pepper.
Add 2 tablespoons of the oil, the wine, cognac, thyme, and
bay leaves. Cover; set aside to marinate for 2 hours at room
temperature.

Remove the beef from the marinade, reserving the marinade,
and pat dry with paper towels.

Preheat the oven to 325°F [165°C]. Cut a piece of parchment
paper into a circle that just fits inside a large Dutch oven or pot.

Place the pot over medium heat and add the pancetta. Cook,
stirring, until the pancetta browns, about 5 minutes; transfer
to a large plate. Increase the heat to medium-high and add
3 tablespoons of the oil to the pot. Once the oil is hot, add the
beef cubes in batches and brown, turning occasionally, until the
cubes are golden brown on all sides, about 5 minutes per batch.
Transfer the meat to the plate with the pancetta.

cont'd

Add the remaining 1 tablespoon of oil to the pot and lower the heat to medium. Add the onions and cook, stirring, until they soften, about 8 minutes. Add the garlic and carrots; season with salt and pepper. Stir to combine, then increase the heat to medium-high. Cook for 5 minutes, then stir in the tomato paste until combined. Add the pancetta, beef, and reserved marinade; stir to combine. Remove the pot from the heat and set the parchment paper circle on top, pressing gently to remove any air bubbles.

Cover the pot with a tight-fitting lid and transfer to the oven. Cook until the meat is extremely tender and the sauce is rich and thick, 3 to 4 hours. Remove from the oven and season. Serve immediately or refrigerate overnight. The next day, skim any hardened fat from the top, and reheat before serving.

Cook the pasta in salted water until al dente. Drain, reserving a bit of the pasta cooking water, then transfer the pasta to a serving bowl. Add the butter and plenty of pepper. Stir in a bit of the reserved pasta water if the pasta looks dry. Sprinkle with the parsley and serve with the daube.

STEAK FOR DIANE

Serves 6

Six 4- to 5-ounce [115 to 140 g] tenderloin filets, pounded to 1 inch [2.5 cm] thick

Fine sea salt

Freshly ground black pepper

3 tablespoons extra-virgin olive oil

4 tablespoons [55 g] unsalted European butter

2 shallots, thinly sliced into rounds

2 garlic cloves, finely chopped

1¼ pounds [570 g] sliced mushrooms, such as cremini, shiitake, and oyster

⅓ cup [80 ml] cognac or brandy

2 tablespoons Dijon mustard

2 tablespoons Worcestershire sauce

⅓ cup [80 ml] heavy cream

½ bunch fresh flat-leaf parsley, coarsely chopped

This is a steak for my mom, Diane. Steak Diane already exists. It is, in fact, a steak, flambéed tableside, which you will have the easiest time finding by getting in a time machine set to 1940s America. And, indeed, my Steak for Diane shares commonalities with the original: thinly pounded steaks, a mushroom cream sauce, and a theatrical (but also please be very careful) blaze of cognac. Mama, this is all for you.

Pat the steaks dry with paper towels and season with salt and pepper.

Heat a large skillet over medium-high heat for 2 minutes. When the skillet is hot, add 2 tablespoons of the oil and 2 tablespoons of the butter. Let the oil warm up, then add the steaks, working in batches as needed. Sear until browned on the first side, about 2 minutes, then flip and sear until browned on the second side. Transfer the steaks to a platter and cover loosely with aluminum foil.

Once all the steaks are cooked, add the remaining 2 tablespoons of butter and 1 tablespoon of oil to the pan and return to medium heat. Add the shallots and cook until tender, about 2 minutes. Add the garlic and cook for 1 minute, then add the mushrooms and season with salt and pepper. Cook, stirring often, until tender and browned, about 5 minutes.

Remove the pan from the heat, tilt it away from you, and pour in the cognac; carefully ignite the alcohol with a long match. Once the fire has died out, stir in the mustard, Worcestershire, and cream. Season with salt and pepper.

Bring to a simmer and cook for 2 minutes, then tuck the steaks and any accumulated juices back into the pan. Cook, turning the steaks in the sauce, until they are cooked to your taste (125°F [52°C] internal temperature is medium-rare) and the sauce is thickened, 2 to 4 minutes. Stir in half the parsley.

Transfer the steaks to plates, spooning the sauce over the top. Sprinkle with the remaining parsley and serve.

LAMB TAGINE

Serves 4 to 6

2 to 3 pounds [910 g to 1.4 kg] boneless lamb shoulder, trimmed and cut into 1½-inch [4 cm] pieces

Fine sea salt

2 to 4 tablespoons [30 to 60 ml] extra-virgin olive oil

2 large yellow onions, thinly sliced

4 garlic cloves, grated on a Microplane

One ½-inch [12 mm] piece fresh ginger, peeled and grated

2 tablespoons tomato paste

1 bay leaf

1 cinnamon stick

1 teaspoon ground cumin

1 teaspoon freshly ground black pepper

¾ teaspoon ground turmeric

Large pinch of saffron

1 cup [140 g] golden raisins

Prepared couscous, for serving (see Note)

½ bunch fresh cilantro, leaves coarsely chopped

Note

To prepare couscous, add 3 cups [540 g] of couscous to a large bowl and pour 3½ cups [840 ml] of boiling water over the top. Stir in ¼ cup [60 ml] of extra-virgin olive oil and 2 teaspoons of fine sea salt; cover and set aside to steam for 3 minutes. Fluff the couscous with a fork, then steam for 2 minutes more. Carefully use your hands to break up any clumps and lightly fluff. Serve warm.

Tagine and other Maghrebi dishes first came to France in the mid-nineteenth century as a result of the country's colonization of North Africa. Cut to the 1970s, when a high influx of immigration to France prompted by government incentives led to the cuisine becoming a beloved part of the French culinary landscape. This dish's technique bears some resemblance to the French ragoût—by which I mean it's a slowly simmered mix of meat and vegetables—but it layers on complexity care of a potent mix of spices and dried fruit. While the modern French dinner table may prefer to forget the horrors of colonization and just enjoy the tagine, food is complicated and I swear you can honor both.

Pat the lamb dry with paper towels and season generously on all sides with salt. Set aside at room temperature for at least 1 hour, or overnight in the refrigerator.

Heat 2 tablespoons of the oil in a large Dutch oven or heavy pot over medium heat. Working in batches, cook the lamb, turning the pieces occasionally, until well browned on all sides, about 10 minutes (adding more oil as needed). Using a slotted spoon, transfer the lamb pieces to a plate and set aside.

Add the onions to the pot and cook until soft, 8 to 10 minutes. Add the garlic and ginger and cook, stirring often, for 2 minutes. Stir in the tomato paste, bay leaf, cinnamon stick, cumin, pepper, turmeric, and saffron and cook, stirring, until the spices are fragrant and the tomato paste starts to darken, about 2 minutes. Return the lamb and any juices on the plate to the pot.

Add the raisins and pour in 4 cups [960 ml] of water. Bring to a boil, then lower the heat to medium-low and bring to a bare simmer. Cover partially and cook, stirring occasionally, for 1 hour and 15 minutes. Remove the lid and continue to cook until the lamb is tender and the sauce has thickened and reduced, 15 to 30 minutes more. Serve with couscous and garnish with cilantro.

SEVEN-HOUR LEG OF LAMB

Serves 6 to 8

One 4- to 5-pound [1.8 to 2.3 kg] leg of lamb

Fine sea salt

Freshly ground black pepper

¼ cup [60 ml] extra-virgin olive oil

1 cup [240 ml] dry rosé wine

1 large yellow onion, diced

8 fresh thyme sprigs

5 garlic cloves, smashed

2 bay leaves

I'm not a lamb person unless it's this leg of lamb. In the classic Provençal preparation, the leg is cooked low and slow with a few aromatics, some red wine, and not much else until the meat is so tender you could eat it with a spoon. In fact, in France you'll find this recipe called either gigot de sept heures (seven-hour lamb) or gigot à la cuillère (lamb with a spoon). Since "spoon lamb" sounds weird as hell, we're sticking with the former—even if this version takes less than seven hours from start to finish.

Preheat the oven to 250°F [120°C].

Season the lamb generously with salt and pepper. Set a roasting pan or a large, rimmed baking sheet over two burners. Turn the heat to medium-high and add the oil. Once the oil is hot, add the lamb and sear until browned on all sides, about 10 minutes. Remove the pan from the heat and transfer the lamb to a large plate; set aside. Pour in the rosé and use a wooden spoon to scrape up any brown bits from the bottom of the pan. Add the onion, thyme, garlic, and bay leaves to the pan. Return the lamb to the pan and roast in the oven until very tender, 4½ to 5 hours. Serve warm.

Carrots with Piment d'Espelette | page 186

Potatoes, Artichokes + Shallots | page 226

(ALMOST) ROYAL COUSCOUS

Serves 8

Stew

3 tablespoons extra-virgin olive oil

1½ pounds [680 g] lamb ribs, cut into pieces

2 pounds [910 g] chicken legs (about 4), legs and thighs separated

8 ounces [230 g] merguez sausages

1 medium yellow onion, finely chopped

1 medium tomato, finely chopped

1 medium red bell pepper, finely chopped

2 garlic cloves, finely chopped

1 bunch fresh cilantro, leaves and stems separated

10 fresh thyme sprigs

1 tablespoon ground cumin

2 teaspoons ground coriander

2 teaspoons sweet paprika

Pinch of cayenne pepper

Fine sea salt

Freshly ground black pepper

1 pound [455 g] carrots (about 8 medium)

8 ounces [230 g] turnips (about 2 medium)

1½ pounds [680 g] zucchini (about 3 medium)

cont'd

If you've eaten couscous royale in Paris, it's likely to have been in a room full of white tablecloths and starched waiters serving from silver platters. Indeed, that was my first experience with the dish early in my Paris years. When I wanted to learn to make it myself, however, I deferred to my best French friend's aunt Isabelle, who herself learned to make the dish with her Algerian father. When she opened the family "cookbook," a leather-bound assemblage of handwritten recipes (some in pencil!), I knew I was in for something infinitely more special than anything from a silver platter.

The dish has roots in North Africa, but the "royale" nomenclature—and any try-hard white-gloved service—is expressly French, catering to upscale Parisian clientele. Regardless of where it's eaten, couscous royale is meant to be celebratory. Technically, to be crowned "royal," there should also be meatballs, lamb chops, and oftentimes skewers of other meat, but a combination of lamb ribs, chicken, and merguez sausage is plenty regal for me, my guests, and my bank account.

To make the stew: In a large Dutch oven or saucepan over medium-high heat, add the oil. Working in batches, brown the lamb ribs, chicken, and sausages, 4 to 5 minutes on each side. Transfer the meat to a plate and set aside.

Drain and reserve the fat from the pan so only about 3 tablespoons remain. Add the onion, tomato, bell pepper, and garlic and stir together with a wooden spoon, scraping up any browned bits from the bottom of the pan. Cook until the onion is translucent, about 5 minutes.

cont'd

Couscous

3 cups [540 g] couscous

¼ cup [60 ml] extra-virgin
olive oil

2 teaspoons fine sea salt

½ cup [70 g] golden raisins

Harissa, for serving

Note

If you can, make the
vegetable and meat mixture
a day ahead of time and
refrigerate overnight. The
next day, use a spoon to
remove the layer of fat that
has risen and solidified on the
top of the pan, then reheat
over low heat before serving.

Use a piece of twine to tie together the cilantro stems and
thyme sprigs. Add to the pan along with the browned meat,
cumin, coriander, paprika, and cayenne. Season with salt and
pepper. Add enough water to come about ½ inch [12 mm]
above the meat and bring to a boil. Lower the heat and simmer
until the meat is tender but not quite falling off the bone, 30 to
40 minutes.

Add the carrots and turnips and cook for 5 minutes, then add
the zucchini and cook until tender, about 10 minutes. Taste
for seasoning.

To make the couscous: Add the couscous to a large bowl and
pour 3½ cups [840 ml] of boiling water over the top. Add the oil
and salt and stir to combine. Cover the bowl with a lid or large
plate and set aside to steam for 3 minutes. Remove the lid and
fluff the couscous with a fork. Cover again and let steam for
another 2 minutes. Carefully use your hands to break up any
clumps in the couscous and lightly fluff. Stir in the raisins.

Serve the couscous with the meat, vegetables, and harissa.

BIGGER BÁNH MÌ

Serves 8

4 carrots, peeled and cut into matchstick-size pieces (about 2 cups [250 g])

1 small daikon, peeled and cut into matchstick-size pieces (about 2 cups [250 g])

1¼ teaspoons fine sea salt

¾ cup [150 g] granulated sugar

¾ cup [180 ml] distilled white vinegar

1¼ pounds [570 g] pork tenderloin, cut across the grain into ½-inch [12 mm] pieces

3 garlic cloves, coarsely chopped

1 lemongrass stalk, trimmed and coarsely chopped

3 tablespoons soy sauce

3 tablespoons fish sauce

2 tablespoons brown sugar

2 to 3 tablespoons vegetable oil

2 baguettes

6 tablespoons [90 g] mayonnaise (see Note, page 115)

6 ounces [170 g] pâté de campagne

1 jalapeño, thinly sliced

1 bunch fresh cilantro, leaves picked

1 seedless cucumber, peeled and sliced into matchsticks

Ground white pepper

Think of French food, and it's unlikely a bánh mì comes immediately to mind, especially a version big enough for a Super Bowl party. But as in most food metropolises across the world, bánh mì is all over Paris. The French colonized Vietnam from 1887 to 1954, brought with them the baguette, and in an unhappy but true eventuality, the modern bánh mì was born. While traditionally a single-serving sandwich, this extra-long version translates the genius of the Vietnamese combination of grilled meat, herbs, pickled vegetables, and pâté to the dinner table.

Combine the carrots and daikon in a colander. Toss with 1 teaspoon of the salt; set aside for 15 minutes. Pat dry with paper towels.

In a large bowl, whisk together the granulated sugar, vinegar, and remaining ¼ teaspoon of salt until the sugar and salt dissolve. Add the carrots and daikon; toss to combine. Set aside at room temperature for 2 hours or refrigerate for up to 5 days.

Sandwich the pork pieces between layers of parchment paper and use a rolling pin to pound them into ¼-inch [6 mm] pieces.

In a shallow baking dish, whisk together the garlic, lemongrass, soy sauce, fish sauce, and brown sugar. Add the pork slices and turn so all sides are soaked in marinade. Set aside for at least 1 hour, or overnight in the refrigerator.

In a large cast-iron skillet or grill pan over medium-high heat, add 1 tablespoon of the vegetable oil and, working in batches, sear each of the marinated pieces until golden on each side, 1 to 2 minutes per side. Transfer to a plate and set aside.

Using a bread knife, cut one end off of each baguette. Slice lengthwise almost all the way through, leaving one long length of the baguette connected (like a hinge) and spread the mayonnaise evenly on the bottom halves of the baguettes. Spread the top halves of the baguettes evenly with pâté. Layer the bottom halves with jalapeño slices, cilantro, cucumber, carrots, and daikon. Arrange a layer of thinly sliced roast pork over the pâté, season with white pepper, and gently press the sandwiches together. Cut into eight pieces and serve immediately.

SAUSAGES WITH FIGS, PLUMS + FENNEL

Serves 6

3 tablespoons extra-virgin olive oil

1 tablespoon grainy mustard

1 pound [455 g] greengage plums, halved and pitted

1 large fennel bulb, halved and thinly sliced

1 large red onion, halved through root end and thinly sliced lengthwise

3 fresh rosemary sprigs

Fine sea salt

Freshly ground black pepper

1½ pounds [680 g] pork sausages (about 8), pricked all over with a sharp paring knife

12 ounces [340 g] fresh figs, stemmed and halved

¼ cup [60 ml] cognac

2 tablespoons unsalted European butter, cut into small pieces

Fig season is the best season, no contest. Extending from the end of summer to the beginning of fall, it also coincides briefly with the magic that is tiny, green-yellow, how-can-they-be-this-sweet greengage plums. Lean into the autumnal half of the season and combine said figs and plums with fennel, sausage, and cognac (you could use verjus [see page 60] here if you're not drinking). This recipe is extremely straightforward to make: Layer some things in a baking dish, roast, add a few more things, roast again, enjoy.

Preheat the oven to 400°F [200°C].

In a small bowl, whisk together the oil and mustard. In a large baking dish or rimmed baking sheet, combine the plums, fennel, onion, and rosemary. Drizzle with the oil-mustard mixture and season with salt and pepper; toss to combine. Roast until the fennel and plums are browned and tender, about 30 minutes.

Add the sausages, figs, and cognac and cook until the liquid is reduced, the sausages are cooked through, and the figs are very tender, 15 to 20 minutes more. Scatter the butter pieces over the sausages and allow to melt. Serve warm.

Gratin Dauphinois | page 229

PORK CHOPS WITH KALE

Serves 6

Six 1-inch [2.5 cm] bone-in pork rib chops (about 12 ounces [340 g] each)

Fine sea salt

Freshly ground black pepper

4 tablespoons [60 ml] extra-virgin olive oil

6 tablespoons [120 g] apricot preserves

¼ cup [60 ml] fresh orange juice

3 tablespoons red wine vinegar

Pinch of red pepper flakes

1 tablespoon Dijon mustard

3 large bunches kale, stemmed and thinly sliced

1 cup [140 g] pitted black olives, such as kalamata, torn

½ cup [70 g] golden raisins

2 tablespoons unsalted European butter, cut into small pieces

There are a lot of really excellent jams, marmalades, and preserves made in France, but a jar of gingham-capped Bonne Maman apricot preserves is the ultimate equalizer. You'll find them everywhere: the corner shop, hotel breakfast buffets, my ex-girlfriend's grandmother's kitchen. You'll also find them at most American grocery stores. Not just for toast, they can and should be used in sweet applications—see (My First) French (Girlfriend's) Apple Tart, page 246—as well as savory (see below).

Preheat the oven to 450°F [230°C] and set a rack in the middle of the oven.

Pat the pork rib chops dry with paper towels and season with salt and pepper.

Heat a large cast-iron or heavy ovenproof skillet over medium-high heat for 2 minutes. When the skillet is hot, add 2 tablespoons of the oil. Add three of the pork chops and sear until browned on the first side, then flip and immediately transfer the skillet to the oven. Continue cooking until an instant-read thermometer inserted horizontally into the center of the meat registers 130°F [54°C], 3 to 5 minutes more, depending on the thickness of the chop. Carefully remove the skillet from the oven, transfer the pork chops to a cutting board, and use a pastry brush to brush the chops with 2 tablespoons of the preserves. Cover loosely with aluminum foil. Repeat with the remaining oil and pork chops and 2 tablespoons of the preserves.

While the pork chops rest, add the orange juice, vinegar, and red pepper flakes to the hot skillet over medium-high heat. Use a wooden spoon to scrape up any browned bits, then stir in the remaining 2 tablespoons of preserves and the mustard. Add the kale in batches to the skillet. Cook, using a pair of tongs to toss the greens often, until all the kale is wilted, 3 to 4 minutes. Add the olives, raisins, and butter and toss. Season and transfer to a serving platter.

Use a sharp knife to cut away the bones from the pork chops; cut into ¼-inch [6 mm] slices. Arrange on top of the greens and serve.

CIDER PORK

Serves 6 to 8

One 2½-pound [1.2 kg] boneless pork loin

Fine sea salt

Freshly ground black pepper

3 tablespoons extra-virgin olive oil

1 large red onion, halved and thinly sliced

4 medium shallots, halved lengthwise and thinly sliced

2 garlic cloves, finely chopped

1½ cups [360 ml] dry hard cider, preferably from Normandy

1½ cups [360 ml] chicken stock, store-bought or homemade

4 fresh thyme sprigs

2 bay leaves

1½ tablespoons whole-grain mustard, plus more for serving

I've never felt more froid de canard—"duck cold" in French, essentially meaning freezing cold—than while cider tasting through Normandy in late November. A reminder, I'm from Wisconsin! It's the kind of damp freeze that sits in your body long after you've left the orchards and drafty warehouses stacked with sweet, fermenting apples and found a fire to sit dangerously close to. This recipe is a product of that rainy, boozy, shivering yet wonderful trip: pork loin laced with cider, aromatics, and mustard, served warm and drunk with more cider, bien sûr.

Preheat the oven to 300°F [150°C].

Season the pork with salt and pepper. Heat the oil in a large Dutch oven over medium heat and brown the pork on all sides, 6 to 8 minutes on each side. Transfer the pork to a plate and add the onion and shallots to the pot. Season with salt and sauté until tender, about 15 minutes. Add the garlic and cook for 3 minutes, then pour in the cider and use a wooden spoon to scrape any browned bits from the bottom of the pot.

Add the stock, thyme, and bay leaves and return the pork to the pot. Cover with a tight-fitting lid and braise in the oven until the meat is tender and registers 145°F [63°C] on a digital thermometer, 1 to 1½ hours.

Transfer the pork loin to a cutting board and set aside to rest. Meanwhile, return the pot to the stove top over medium-high heat. Bring to a boil and cook, stirring, until the sauce reduces by half, 10 to 15 minutes. Stir in the mustard and season with salt and pepper.

Slice the pork and serve with the onion-cider sauce and additional grainy mustard.

Extremely French Carrot Salad | page 215

CASSOULET

Serves 6 to 8

1 pound [455 g] dried white beans, preferably Tarbais or cannellini, picked over, soaked overnight, and drained

2 large yellow onions, one peeled and left whole, one finely chopped

1 whole clove

12 ounces [340 g] garlic sausage or kielbasa, cut into three pieces

2 medium carrots, cut in half crosswise

2 celery stalks, cut in half crosswise

6 fresh flat-leaf parsley sprigs

3 fresh thyme sprigs

2 bay leaves

Freshly ground black pepper

Fine sea salt

8 cups [2 L] very good or homemade stock

4 legs duck confit (about 2 pounds [910 g])

6 ounces [170 g] pancetta, cut crosswise into ¼-inch [6 mm] strips

2¼ pounds [1 kg] pork or lamb ribs

1 pound [455 g] mild pork sausage

4 garlic cloves, minced

There are fun, last-minute, *come over for dinner!* nights and then there's cassoulet night. Please don't be intimidated. For all the pomp built around it, cassoulet is a simple bean and meat dish deeply rooted in French home cooking. It does take a long time to execute, so maybe save it for a long weekend and your favorite meat-loving friends.

Three cities in southwest France—Carcassonne, Toulouse, and Castelnaudary—have been fighting over claim to a vrai ("real") cassoulet since the nineteenth century. In 1966, a general recipe of sorts for said "real" cassoulet was codified by a French organization called the États Généraux de la Gastronomie Français and mandates that as long as the stew consists of at least 30 percent pork, mutton, or preserved duck or goose (or a combination of the three), and 70 percent white beans and stock, fresh pork rinds, herbs, and flavorings, it can be called cassoulet. This formula leaves room for all three cities—and you!—to lay claim to the real thing. It's all very pedantic and French and I love it.

I learned to make vrai cassoulet at a friend's family home in Carcassonne. This recipe incorporates much of what I learned, while balancing what's reasonable for a modern home cook. I skip, for example, lining the bottom of the dish with pork skin but follow my cassoulet guide's strict instruction not to put tomatoes in or bread crumbs on top. I am well aware that Julia Child used both, and while I hate to cross swords with Our Lady of Americans Cooking French Food, I say stick with tradition.

Preparation is the name of the cassoulet game, and the number one hardest thing about making a cassoulet when you're not in southwest France is shopping for the ingredients. So shop in advance, then take a day to soak the beans, a day to cook the soaked beans, and a final day to assemble and bake the whole damn thing.

Rinse the drained beans and add to a medium pot. Pierce the whole peeled onion with a clove and add to the pot along with the garlic sausage, carrots, and celery. Use a piece of kitchen twine to tie together the parsley, thyme, and bay leaves and add to the pot. Season generously with pepper and a small pinch of salt (the duck confit and pancetta will add more salt later, so you don't want to oversalt at the beginning). Add the stock and any additional water to cover the beans by 2 inches [5 cm] and bring to a boil over medium-high heat. Lower the heat to a simmer and cook, skimming any scum that rises to the top of the beans, until they are tender but still hold their shape, about 2 hours. (If you're using cannellini beans, the cook time will be shorter.)

Remove the pot from the heat and remove and discard the garlic sausage pieces, onion, carrots, celery, and herb bundle. Strain and reserve the beans and broth separately.

Preheat the oven to 300°F [150°C].

In a large Dutch oven or pot over medium heat, add the duck legs and cook to render the fat and lightly brown, 8 to 10 minutes. Transfer the legs to a plate. Add the pancetta to the duck fat and cook, stirring, until browned, 6 to 8 minutes. Use a slotted spoon to transfer the mixture to the beans. Stir to combine. Add the ribs, working in batches as necessary, and brown on all sides, 5 to 6 minutes per side. Transfer to the platter with the duck legs. Finally, add the pork sausage and cook until browned on just one side, about 6 minutes; transfer to the platter.

Carefully remove all but 6 tablespoons [90 ml] of the duck fat from the pot (reserve the rest for future use) and return the pot to medium heat. Add the finely chopped onion and cook, stirring with a wooden spoon to scrape up any browned bits from the bottom of the pot, until the onions are translucent, about 3 minutes. Add the garlic and cook for 1 minute more. Season very generously with pepper and remove the pot from the heat.

Use a slotted spoon to transfer half of the bean mixture to a 5- to 6-quart [4.7 to 5.7 L] earthenware casserole dish or a Dutch oven. Arrange the duck confit pieces on top. Drizzle with half of the onion–duck fat mixture. Add the ribs, cover with the remaining beans, and top with the sausages. Use a ladle to add just enough of the bean cooking liquid to come up to the top of the beans but not completely cover them. Use water if you run out of the bean cooking broth (reserve any remaining broth if you don't). Drizzle with the rest of the onion–duck fat mixture.

Bake until a skin starts to form on top of the cassoulet, 1½ to 2 hours. Use the back of the ladle to gently break the crust in a few spots and ladle more of the reserved cooking liquid or water over the top as needed. Return to the oven and continue breaking the crust and adding more liquid (use water if you run out of bean cooking liquid) every 30 minutes five more times (until you break the crust a total of seven times . . . this is officially a potion recipe now). Continue cooking until a deeply brown, thick crust forms, 30 minutes to 1½ hours more. Serve warm.

MUSSELS WITH ROSÉ + HEIRLOOM TOMATOES

Serves 4 to 6

4 pounds [1.8 kg] mussels

3 tablespoons extra-virgin olive oil

2 medium shallots, finely chopped

6 garlic cloves, finely chopped

1½ pounds [680 g] heirloom tomatoes, coarsely chopped

1 fresh basil sprig, plus ½ cup [20 g] coarsely chopped fresh basil

½ teaspoon red pepper flakes

Fine sea salt

1 cup [240 ml] dry rosé wine

Frites (page 224) or crusty bread, for serving

This is the kind of recipe you decide to make during tomato season because it sounds pretty good and easy and budget-friendly, and then you make it once a week for dinner for the next month because it's *extremely* good and easy and budget-friendly. Prep everything in advance, ask your friends to bring rosé, use part of one bottle to make the dish, and pour the rest when you serve the meal 12 minutes later.

Place the mussels in a colander or fine-mesh sieve and rinse with cold water. Scrub gently to remove any grit and use your hands to remove the "beard" (the thread-like piece attached to the side of the shells) by tugging firmly. If any mussels are open and don't close when tapped, discard them. Drain and transfer to a large bowl.

In a large pot or Dutch oven over medium heat, add the oil. Once the oil is hot, add the shallots and garlic and cook, stirring, until the shallots are translucent, about 5 minutes. Add the chopped tomatoes, basil sprig, and red pepper flakes and cook for 3 minutes. Season with salt and pour in the rosé. Let simmer, uncovered, for 5 minutes.

Add the mussels to the pot and use a wooden spoon to stir them into the tomato mixture. Cover the pot and cook, stirring halfway through, until the mussels are opened and fully cooked, 5 to 8 minutes.

When the mussels are opened, uncover the pot and remove from the heat. Season with salt as needed, sprinkle with chopped basil, and serve with frites or crusty bread.

CLAMS WITH SHERRY + OLIVES

Serves 4 to 6

3 tablespoons extra-virgin olive oil

6 garlic cloves, finely chopped

1 teaspoon piment d'Espelette

Fine sea salt

3 pounds [1.4 kg] small clams, such as littlenecks, scrubbed clean

1 cup [160 g] Castelvetrano olives

1 cup [240 ml] dry white wine

½ cup [120 ml] fino or manzanilla sherry

½ cup [20 g] finely chopped fresh flat-leaf parsley

Crusty bread, for serving

Consider these clams your excuse to ensure you keep two essential non-French items in house: dry Spanish sherry and buttery Italian olives. The complex flavor of the dish—briny, aromatic, slightly spicy—belies the extraordinarily simple method of actually making it. Please don't be shy with the amount of bread you serve alongside—the clams are delicious, but the broth created by their nectar mixed with the aforementioned sherry and olives is the real reason for the season.

In a large Dutch oven or pot over medium-high heat, add the oil and garlic and cook, stirring, until the garlic is golden and fragrant, about 2 minutes. Add the piment d'Espelette and season with salt; cook for 10 seconds more, then stir in the clams, olives, wine, and sherry. Bring to a boil, then cover the pot with a tight-fitting lid, lower the heat to medium-low, and simmer until the clams open, 10 to 12 minutes. Uncover, remove and discard any clams that don't open, and add ¼ cup [10 g] of the parsley to the pot. Stir to combine and transfer to a serving platter. Sprinkle with the remaining ¼ cup [10 g] of parsley. Serve with crusty bread.

FRENCH SHRIMP BOIL

Serves 6 to 8

1 tablespoon plus
2 teaspoons herbes de
Provence

1½ teaspoons freshly
ground black pepper

1¼ teaspoons sweet paprika

1 teaspoon flaky sea salt

2 pounds [910 g] small, red-
skinned potatoes

8 baby artichokes, turned
(see Note)

4 garlic cloves, smashed

2 tablespoons white wine
vinegar

1 tablespoon Dijon mustard

4 fresh thyme sprigs

2 bay leaves

1½ teaspoons fine sea salt

Pinch of cayenne pepper

2 cups [480 ml] dry white
wine

2 lemons

1½ pounds [680 g] head-on,
tail-on jumbo shrimp or
prawns

Mayonnaise (see Note,
page 115), for serving

Unsalted European butter,
for serving

Radishes, for serving

Crusty bread, for serving

Note

To turn artichokes, pull off the
outer leaves; trim the end of the
stems and 1 inch [2.5 cm] off
the tops. Use a peeler to shave
off the dark layer of the stem.
Halve lengthwise; scoop out
the choke; discard. Keep in
lemon water until ready to use.

When I was younger, my mom had one of those little ceramic pots from Williams-Sonoma with "Herbes de Provence" written in script. Ten-year-old me thought it was peak chic. While we rarely used the mix of thyme, basil, savory, fennel, and lavender flowers, saving it instead for "special" dishes that were few and far between, twenty years later the exact same pot remains in her spice cabinet, now refreshed with herbs brought back from Provence. I wish we had had this recipe then. A Frenchified take on a low-country boil (or a New England clambake), a French shrimp boil is communal eating at its finest, best piled over newspaper, avec beaucoup d'amis and napkins on hand.

In a small dish, combine 1 tablespoon of herbes de Provence, ½ teaspoon of black pepper, ¼ teaspoon of paprika, and the flaky salt. Set aside.

In a large pot, combine the potatoes, artichokes, garlic, vinegar, mustard, thyme, bay leaves, the remaining 2 teaspoons of the herbes de Provence, the fine sea salt, the remaining 1 teaspoon of black pepper, the remaining 1 teaspoon of paprika, and the cayenne. Add the wine and 6 cups [1.4 L] of water to the pot. Halve one of the lemons, squeeze the juice from both halves into the pot, and add the halves. Bring to a boil over high heat, then lower the heat and simmer until the potatoes and artichokes are fork tender, 10 to 12 minutes.

Add the shrimp to the simmering water and cook until the shells are bright red and the meat is slightly opaque and just cooked through, 3 to 4 minutes.

Immediately strain the mixture through a colander; discard the lemon halves. Spread the shrimp, potatoes, and artichokes on platters or a newspaper-lined table. Cut the remaining lemon into wedges. Serve immediately with the lemon wedges, prepared herbes de Provence–salt mixture, mayonnaise, butter, radishes, and crusty bread.

EASIER BOUILLABAISSE

Serves 6 to 8

Broth

½ cup [120 ml] extra-virgin olive oil

2 large yellow onions, chopped

1 medium fennel bulb, chopped, plus 6 fennel fronds

4 garlic cloves, smashed

One 2-inch [5 cm] piece orange zest, or ½ teaspoon dried orange peel

6 fresh flat-leaf parsley sprigs

2 fresh thyme sprigs

1 bay leaf

2 large pinches of saffron threads

Pinch of cayenne pepper

3 large tomatoes, peeled, seeded, and chopped

2½ to 3 pounds [1.2 to 1.4 kg] whole fish and/or fish bones and heads (see Note)

2 cups [480 ml] dry white wine

¼ cup [60 ml] pastis

Fine sea salt

Freshly ground black pepper

cont'd

Some say bouillabaisse is only bouillabaisse if you have it in Marseille. Those are likely the people selling . . . bouillabaisse in Marseille (or else people who have been to Marseille and are real annoying about it). To be clear, you can have a truly transformative bouillabaisse in the gritty, crazy, completely intoxicating port city where it was born, but—as is true for all "must eat" things anywhere—you can also get a really shitty one. I've had both.

Regardless of where you live, there are, however, a few rules to consider when making bouillabaisse.

Rule one, which I break every time: Bouillabaisse should be served in two separate courses—first as a soup and second with the seafood cooked and served in the broth.

Rule two, which I never break: Serving bouillabaisse with rouille is nonnegotiable. The first time I ate bouillabaisse—yes, in Marseille—I had no idea what to do with the garlicky, mayo-like spread thickened with bread crumbs and set on the table with small toasted breads before our meal came out. My friend and I ended up eating it as a relatively mediocre snack until we were told in no uncertain terms by our waiter to spread the bread with rouille, set it in the bottom of the bowl, and ladle the hot broth over the top. It's the opposite of mediocre (as is most soup poured atop bread). So, definitely do that.

Rule three, which is also worth abiding: There should be a minimum of four types of seafood in your bouillabaisse. For flavor and texture and visual appeal, all yes, but also, if you're gonna make bouillabaisse, you might as well actually make bouillabaisse.

Bonus rule: Bouillabaisse must be made with rascasse (also called scorpion fish). Some say this spectacularly spiny fish is found only in the Mediterranean; others firmly disagree. If I have the energy and can find rascasse in Paris, I'll use it. If you can't, that is certainly not a reason to avoid making bouillabaisse altogether.

cont'd

Bouillabaisse

5 pounds [2.3 kg] mixed whole and filleted fish (see Note)

Fine sea salt

Freshly ground black pepper

1 pound [455 g] mussels, rinsed, scrubbed, and beards removed

1 baguette, thinly sliced and toasted

Quick Rouille or Quicker Rouille (recipes follow)

Note

Ask your fish gal for fish bones and heads—they often have plenty extra and will sell them for cheap or just give them to you. For the broth, try for less expensive whole fish, such as rockfish, monkfish, or red snapper. If you're using whole fish, cut them into big chunks before adding to the pot.

À TABLE

Note

For the poached fish, ask your fishmonger to help you pick the freshest mix you can find and go for a mix of whole fish and fillets. Variety matters to the complex flavor of the finished dish, so try to get a mix of firm and delicate, oily and lean fish. Sea bass (like branzino), sea bream (durade or porgy), cod, haddock, hake, halibut, sea trout, snapper, John Dory, Dover sole, monkfish, etc. etc. all work. Ask your fishmonger to clean and scale any whole fish and save heads, bones, and trimmings for your broth.

To make the broth: In a large Dutch oven over medium heat, add the oil. Once the oil is hot, add the onions, fennel bulbs and fronds, garlic, orange zest, parsley, thyme, bay leaf, saffron, and cayenne. Cook, stirring, until the onion and fennel are soft, 10 to 15 minutes. Add the tomatoes and cook, stirring, for 3 minutes. Add the fish and stir to combine.

Pour in the wine and pastis and use a wooden spoon to scrape any browned bits from the bottom of the pot. Increase the heat to high and boil for 2 minutes. Add 12 cups [2.8 L] of hot water and bring back to a boil. Lower the heat to a simmer and cook, uncovered, until the broth is reduced by a quarter, 30 to 45 minutes. Season with salt and pepper. Strain through a fine-mesh sieve, pressing on the solids before discarding. Set the broth aside to cool. Broth can be made 1 day ahead; if making ahead, allow it to cool, then refrigerate, covered, for up to 1 day.

To make the bouillabaisse: Return the broth to the heat and bring to a very gentle simmer. Starting with the larger whole fish, season with salt and pepper and add to the broth (the fish should be fully submerged, so work in batches as needed). Poach until the fish are just cooked through and, as each is cooked, transfer to a serving platter. Season the fillets and repeat until all the fish are cooked.

Once all the fish are cooked, add the mussels and cook until they have just opened, 5 to 8 minutes. Transfer the mussels to the serving platter.

To serve, bring the pot of hot broth and the platter of fish and mussels to the table. Divide the fish and mussels among bowls and top with hot broth. Serve with toasts and rouille.

QUICK ROUILLE

Makes about ¾ cup [200 g]

¾ cup [45 g] coarse, day-old bread crumbs

1 large roasted red bell pepper, peeled and seeded (see Note)

2 garlic cloves, grated on a Microplane

Pinch of cayenne pepper

Fine sea salt

¼ cup [60 ml] extra-virgin olive oil

In the bowl of a food processor, add the bread crumbs and pour 2 tablespoons of warm water over the top. Add the bell pepper, garlic, and cayenne, season with salt, and process until a paste forms. With the food processor running, add the oil in a slow, steady stream until all the oil is added and the mixture is thick and mayonnaise-like in consistency. Store, covered, in the refrigerator for up to 4 days.

QUICKER ROUILLE

Makes about ¾ cup [200 g]

½ cup [120 g] mayonnaise (see Note, page 115)

1 large roasted red bell pepper, finely chopped (see Note)

2 garlic cloves, grated on a Microplane

Pinch of cayenne pepper

Fine sea salt

In a small bowl, stir together the mayonnaise, bell pepper, garlic, and cayenne. Season with salt. Store, covered, in the refrigerator for up to 4 days.

Note

There are two ways to roast peppers: on the stove top and in the oven. I prefer the stove top, but I—and the bulk of Parisian apartments—have an induction cooktop, so that method is often reserved for vacation cooking and when I'm in my mom's big, beautiful midwestern kitchen.

Broiler method: Preheat the broiler. Halve the bell peppers; remove and discard the core, stem, and seeds. Place on a baking sheet, cut-sides down, and drizzle with a small amount of olive oil. Broil until the skins are black, 10 to 12 minutes. Remove the peppers and set aside to cool slightly. Turn the oven to 250°F [120°C].

Use your hands to remove the charred skins from the peppers and return the peppers to the baking sheet. Bake until they are tender, 20 to 30 minutes, then let cool and slice into strips.

Stove-top method: Turn the flame to medium and place each of the peppers directly on a burner. Use tongs to rotate often until the skin is blackened all over, 10 to 12 minutes. Transfer to a large bowl and cover with an upside-down plate or baking sheet to steam for 10 minutes. Remove the peppers from the bowl, and remove and discard the core, stem, seeds, and blackened skin; slice into strips.

NIÇOISE (FOR A CROWD)

Serves 6 to 8

Vinaigrette

2 anchovies, finely chopped

1 garlic clove, finely chopped

Fine sea salt

3 tablespoons fresh lemon juice

1 tablespoon Dijon mustard

1 teaspoon mild honey

½ cup [120 ml] extra-virgin olive oil

Freshly ground black pepper

Salad

6 large eggs

8 ounces [230 g] haricots verts or green beans, trimmed

1 pound [455 g] small waxy potatoes

5 cups [100 g] frisée, mâche, or other tender greens

Fine sea salt

Freshly ground black pepper

Two 6-ounce [170 g] cans tuna packed in olive oil, drained

2 cups [320 g] cherry tomatoes, halved

2 small seedless cucumbers, sliced into ¼-inch [6 mm] slices

5 small radishes, sliced into rounds

¾ cup [120 g] Niçoise olives

¼ cup [30 g] salted capers, soaked, rinsed, and drained

Flaky sea salt

This is a "choose your own adventure" salad and the ideal meal for a crowd: It can all be prepped in advance, and instead of coming together in one big bowl, each component—beans, greens, potatoes—is dressed with the vinaigrette separately, and then arranged on the plate ingredient by ingredient. It sounds fussy, but when you and your fellow diners are picking and choosing your preferred tuna-to-greens-to-beans ratio, you'll be happy you fussed.

To make the vinaigrette: Using the flat side of a knife, smash together the anchovies, garlic, and a pinch of salt until a thick paste forms. Transfer to a small bowl and stir in the lemon juice, mustard, and honey. Slowly add the oil, whisking until the vinaigrette is emulsified; season with salt and pepper.

To make the salad: Prepare an ice bath in a large bowl and set aside. Bring a large pot of salted water to a boil. Gently add the eggs and cook for 7 minutes. Using a slotted spoon, transfer the eggs to the prepared ice bath and chill until cold, about 5 minutes. Peel the eggs and set aside. Refresh the ice bath with more ice.

Add the haricots verts to the same pot of boiling water and cook until just tender, 2 to 4 minutes. Use tongs to transfer to the ice bath; chill, then pat dry and transfer to a bowl. Toss with one-fourth of the prepared dressing. Add the potatoes to the boiling water. Cook until fork tender, 10 to 15 minutes. Drain through a sieve and transfer the warm potatoes to a bowl; toss with half of the remaining dressing.

To serve, arrange the greens on a large platter; season with salt and pepper. Drizzle with the remainder of the prepared dressing. Halve the eggs and arrange along with the tuna, potatoes, haricots verts, tomatoes, cucumbers, radishes, olives, and capers in separate piles on top of the lettuce. Sprinkle with flaky salt and serve.

CASSE-CROÛTE TUNISIAN

Serves 6

1 cucumber (about
8 ounces [230 g]), peeled
and finely chopped

1 tomato, finely chopped

½ small white onion, finely
chopped

8 tablespoons [120 ml]
extra-virgin olive oil

Fine sea salt

Freshly ground black
pepper

8 ounces [230 g] Yukon
gold potatoes (about
2 medium)

6 large eggs

3 tablespoons harissa

3 fresh baguettes, split
lengthwise

Flaky sea salt

Two 8-ounce [230 g] jars
tuna packed in oil, drained
and roughly flaked

¾ cup [120 g] oil-cured
black olives, pitted and
halved

Note

While most of the recipes in
this book are written to be
eaten . . . à table, that doesn't
mean you can't expand your
definition of what a table
looks like. Many recipes, like
say Casse-Croûte Tunisian,
Bigger Bánh Mì (page 133),
Ratatouille (page 161), Tomato
Tart (page 166), or a number
of the sides in the following
section, make excellent
choices when the weather
is too nice to be anywhere
but outside.

While I'm sure this sandwich is delicious as a snack, which
is colloquially what "casse-croûte" means, I'm into it as a
meal. Casse-croûte is the North African take on France's pan
bagnat (a traditional tuna and vegetable sandwich from Nice),
the product of French rule in Tunisia first as an occupation in
1881, then a "protectorate" until full independence in 1956.
The "snack" is a hunger-satisfying combination of tinned tuna,
potatoes, eggs, olives, peppers, and harissa, often built on a
crusty white roll in Tunisia. In Paris, it's common to find both
the traditional roll and a French baguette, used here.

In a medium bowl, stir together the cucumber, tomato, and
onion. Drizzle with 2 tablespoons of the oil and season with
salt and pepper. Set aside to marinate.

Prepare an ice bath in a large bowl and set aside. Bring a
medium pot of salted water to a boil over high heat. Add the
potatoes and cook for 18 minutes, then carefully add the eggs
and continue to cook for 7 minutes. Use a slotted spoon to
transfer the eggs to the ice bath. Use a sharp paring knife to
check the potatoes; once they are easily pierced, transfer
to the ice bath as well.

Peel and slice the cooled eggs and potatoes. In a small bowl,
whisk together the harissa with 3 tablespoons of the oil.
Spread one side of each baguette with 2 tablespoons of the
harissa–olive oil mixture. Drizzle the other side of each baguette
with 1 tablespoon of the oil and sprinkle with flaky salt. On the
harissa side of each baguette, evenly spread ⅔ cup [150 g] of
the tomato-onion-cucumber mixture. Divide the tuna between
the baguettes and top each evenly with egg and potato slices.
Finish with the olives, close each sandwich, and slice each in
half before serving.

SEAFOOD PLATTER

Serves 6

Court Bouillon

1 cup [240 ml] dry white wine

½ cup [120 ml] white wine vinegar

2 medium yellow onions, chopped

2 medium carrots, peeled and chopped

1 garlic clove, smashed

2 tablespoons fine sea salt

1 tablespoon whole peppercorns

1 tablespoon whole coriander seeds

4 fresh thyme sprigs

2 bay leaves

1 lemon, halved

Seafood Platter

1 pound [455 g] large shrimp (16 to 20), deveined

One 1-pound [455 g] lobster (optional)

One 1- to 2-pound [455 to 910 g] crab (optional)

1 pound [455 g] mussels and/or clams

18 oysters

12 ounces [340 g] smoked fish, such as smoked salmon, trout, or sable

1 small tin fish roe (optional, see Note)

Mignonette (page 91), for serving

Mayonnaise (see Note, page 115), for serving

Lemon wedges, for serving

Fresh herb sprigs, such as dill, parsley, and chives, for serving

Some of my best memories in France have been made in direct proximity to a seafood platter. Found in tiny shacks and grand restaurants alike on any of France's coasts, mounds of recently caught, local shellfish and bivalves are piled over ice on platters, in tiered layers, or, if you've found yourself in an especially touristy spot, atop a ceramic boat.

Questionable serving vessels aside, seafood platters can and should be fully customized to season, taste, and budget. When serving a crowd, I pull out the impossibly big, beautiful vintage silver platter I found years ago at a flea market and now keep on the top of the highest kitchen cabinet, because when else am I going to use it? If you happen to have one of these, this is the time; if you don't, please don't get precious about it and use whatever platters, plates, or pie tins you have and double or triple them up as needed.

In terms of seafood variety, you can certainly go big, although I prefer to choose a few favorites, lean generously into portion size, and splurge on a tin of fish roe. To that end, I've tailored this recipe with an eye toward the common seafood platter players, but do adjust according to what you like and what you can find (as ever!). For anything that needs cooking, poach separately in the court bouillon (in French, "fast stock"), then chill for at least 1 hour and up to a day in advance. As for everything else, just make sure it's extra fresh and keep it on ice (see the headnote on page 91 for how to crush your own). Last thing: Traditionally, seafood platters are served in France as appetizers, but with a salad and enough bread, butter, and intent, it shall be a main.

To make the court bouillon: In a large pot over high heat, combine 8 cups [2 L] of water, the wine, vinegar, onions, carrots, garlic, salt, peppercorns, coriander, thyme, and bay leaves. Squeeze the lemon halves into the pot, then add the halves. Bring to a boil, then lower the heat and simmer for 15 minutes. Strain the liquid through a fine-mesh sieve, pressing lightly on the vegetables to extract the flavors; discard the solids. Use the bouillon immediately or refrigerate, covered, for 2 days (or freeze for up to 1 month).

If you have a caviar budget, by all means. If not, I love a small tin of salmon or trout roe. They add an indulgent vibe without putting you in credit card debt.

To make the seafood platter: Set aside 1 cup [240 ml] of the court bouillon for cooking the mussels and/or clams (or 2 cups [480 ml] if you're cooking both). Return the remaining court bouillon to a boil and cook the seafood in this order: Add the shrimp and cook until lightly pink and no longer translucent, about 2 minutes. Use a slotted spoon to transfer the shrimp to a platter or rimmed baking sheet to cool. Add the lobster (if using), and boil for 5 to 10 minutes (the lobster should be bright red and the internal temperature 135°F to 140°F [57°C to 60°C]). Remove the pot from the heat and let sit for 10 minutes. Use a pair of tongs and transfer the lobster to the baking sheet with the shrimp to cool. Bring the bouillon back to a boil and add the crab (if using). Cover the pot, adjust the heat to a simmer, and cook for 15 minutes. Transfer the crab to the baking sheet with the shrimp and lobster and let cool at room temperature for 30 minutes, then transfer the baking sheet to the refrigerator and chill for at least 1 hour and up to overnight.

To cook the mussels and/or clams, add 1 cup [240 ml] of the reserved court bouillon to a large skillet and bring to a boil. Add the mussels or clams (if using both, cook them separately in their own 1 cup [240 ml] of court bouillon) and cover the pan. Cook until all the shells have opened, about 5 minutes. Transfer to a baking sheet and cool completely.

To serve, arrange the chilled seafood and shellfish on a platter. Use an oyster knife to open the oysters and arrange on the platter along with the smoked fish and tin of fish roe (if using). Serve with mignonette, mayonnaise, lemon wedges, and herbs.

RATATOUILLE

Serves 6

2 small eggplants, cut into
½-inch [12 mm] dice

2 teaspoons fine sea salt,
plus more as needed

12 tablespoons [180 ml]
extra-virgin olive oil

2 medium zucchini, cut into
½-inch [12 mm] dice

Freshly ground black
pepper

1 large yellow onion, cut
into ½-inch [12 mm] dice

1 bunch fresh basil tied
in a bouquet with kitchen
twine, plus 2 tablespoons
chopped fresh basil

6 garlic cloves, finely
chopped

2 medium red bell peppers,
seeded and cut into ½-inch
[12 mm] dice

4 medium plum tomatoes,
cut into ½-inch [12 mm]
dice, or one 14-ounce
[400 g] can plum tomatoes

Pinch of red pepper flakes

One summer, several years back, a couple of nights of ratatouille throw-down at peak season turned into a month of ratatouille, crossing two European countries. Those ratatouilles ranged from traditional, to make-it-breakfast-with-an-egg, to throw-it-all-in-the-blender-and-call-it-a-dip. My ex-girlfriend—the throw-down competition—always made a more golden, oilier, spicier ratatouille than I, which I secretly loved but pretended to just like, so credit where credit is due: Here is her recipe. I ate it for a month straight; it's *really* good.

Toss the diced eggplant with the salt. Transfer to a colander and set aside to drain for about 20 minutes. Use paper towels to pat the eggplant dry.

Set a large skillet over medium heat and add 4 tablespoons [60 ml] of the oil. Once the oil is hot, add the eggplant and cook, stirring frequently, until the eggplant is golden on all sides and tender, about 20 minutes. Transfer the eggplant to a large bowl.

In the same pan, heat 2 tablespoons of the oil. Add the zucchini and season lightly with salt and pepper. Cook, stirring often, until the zucchini is browned and soft, 8 to 10 minutes. Transfer to the bowl with the eggplant.

Heat 2 tablespoons of the oil and add the onion. Cook, stirring occasionally, until the onion is soft, 8 to 10 minutes. Stir in the basil bouquet and the garlic and season with salt. Add the bell peppers and cook, stirring often, until the peppers are very tender and the onion is golden, 10 to 12 minutes. Transfer to the bowl with the zucchini and eggplant.

Add 2 tablespoons of the oil, the tomatoes, and red pepper flakes to the pan. Season with salt. Cook, stirring occasionally, until most of the liquid evaporates, about 15 minutes. Return the rest of the vegetables to the pan and continue to cook for another 5 minutes. Remove from the heat and set aside to cool slightly. Finish by drizzling with the remaining 2 tablespoons of oil.

Serve warm or at room temperature.

SUMMER TIAN

Serves 4 to 6

8 tablespoons [120 ml] extra-virgin olive oil

2 large yellow onions, thinly sliced

6 garlic cloves, finely chopped

1 tablespoon finely chopped fresh thyme leaves

Fine sea salt

Freshly ground black pepper

2 large zucchini, cut into ¼-inch [6 mm] rounds

2 small eggplants, cut into ¼-inch [6 mm] rounds

3 large tomatoes, cored and cut into ¼-inch [6 mm] slices

Don't get me wrong, I love the 2007 Disney classic *Ratatouille*. A rat! Cooking! But that last dish, that inspired, layered reinterpretation of ratatouille that cracks open the restaurant critic's hardened heart is . . . not ratatouille. It's a tian, and tian is and has been a dish in its own right on Provençal tables for generations. The word "tian" is used for both a shallow earthenware baking dish as well as the recipe traditionally baked inside it, and that often means alternating rows of thinly sliced vegetables. In the case of this recipe—and Remy's—those vegetables mirror the ones found in classic ratatouille.

Preheat the oven to 350°F [180°C].

In a large skillet over medium-high heat, add 2 tablespoons of the oil. When the oil is hot, add the onions and cook until they begin to soften, about 5 minutes. Add the garlic and thyme and season with salt and pepper. Cook for another 5 minutes, then transfer the onion-garlic mixture to a 9-by-13-inch [23 by 33 cm] baking dish.

Drizzle with 2 tablespoons of the oil. Start to make rows of zucchini, eggplant, and tomatoes across the dish, standing each slice up on one end and overlapping the slices, making sure to pack the rows tightly together. Continue until the baking dish is filled. Season with salt and pepper and drizzle with 2 tablespoons of the oil.

Cover the dish tightly with aluminum foil and bake until the vegetables start to soften, 30 to 35 minutes. Remove the foil and increase the oven temperature to 400°F [200°C]. Continue to bake until the vegetables are very soft, 20 to 30 minutes more. Remove the dish from the oven, drizzle with the remaining 2 tablespoons of oil, and serve warm or at room temperature.

WINTER TIAN

Serves 6 to 8

6 tablespoons [90 ml] extra-virgin olive oil

2 tablespoons unsalted European butter

1 medium red onion, halved and thinly sliced

3 garlic cloves, finely chopped

12 ounces [340 g] mixed mushrooms, such as cremini, shiitake, and maitake, thinly sliced

Fine sea salt

Freshly ground black pepper

2 tablespoons red wine vinegar

½ teaspoon red pepper flakes

1 small butternut squash, peeled, seeded, and cut into thin half-moons

12 ounces [340 g] Yukon gold potatoes, thinly sliced into rounds

2 medium sweet potatoes, thinly sliced into rounds

10 large sage leaves, finely chopped

Winter tian exists to fill the void of the ten months a year we spend *not* in peak tomato/zucchini/eggplant season. If you are in that blessed season—or Southern California—flip back a page. If not, here are my loving condolences in recipe form.

Preheat the oven to 400°F [200°C].

In a large skillet over medium-high heat, add 2 tablespoons of the oil and the butter. When the butter is melted, add the onion and cook, stirring occasionally, until tender, about 10 minutes. Add the garlic and mushrooms and season with salt and black pepper. Cook, stirring often, until the mushrooms are tender and their liquid releases, about 8 minutes. Add 1 tablespoon of the vinegar and cook until the liquid reduces, about 2 minutes. Stir in ¼ teaspoon of the red pepper flakes and cook for another 30 seconds. Transfer the onion-mushroom mixture to a 9-by-13-inch [23 by 33 cm] baking dish.

Start to make rows of squash, potatoes, and sweet potatoes across the dish, standing each slice up on one end and overlapping the slices, making sure to pack the rows tightly together. Continue until the baking dish is filled. Season with salt and black pepper and drizzle with 2 tablespoons of the oil.

Cover the dish tightly with aluminum foil and bake until the vegetables start to soften, 30 to 35 minutes. Remove the foil and continue to bake until the vegetables are very tender and lightly golden, 30 to 40 minutes more.

In a small bowl, whisk together the sage, the remaining 2 tablespoons of oil, 1 tablespoon of vinegar, and ¼ teaspoon of red pepper flakes. Season with salt and pepper and pour evenly over the hot tian. Serve warm or at room temperature.

TOMATO TART

Makes one
9-inch [23 cm] tart

1½ cups [210 g] all-purpose flour

1 teaspoon fine sea salt, plus more as needed

2 teaspoons finely chopped fresh chives

½ cup [110 g] cold unsalted European butter, cut into ¼-inch [6 mm] cubes

3 small heirloom tomatoes, sliced into ¾-inch [2 cm] rounds

½ cup [120 g] crème fraîche

Freshly ground black pepper

Flaky sea salt

Note

You will have extra tart dough and you should not waste it. Gently gather the extra pieces into a ball and roll out into a piece ¼ inch [6 mm] thick. Brush with a bit of olive oil and season generously with flaky salt and freshly ground black pepper. Bake at 400°F [200°C] until very golden, about 20 minutes. Snack on it warm with or without extra crème fraîche.

To bolster your chances of leftovers for breakfast—trust me, you'll want them—serve this tomato tart with a salad and a few sides. Better yet, just make two.

In a medium bowl, whisk together the flour, ½ teaspoon of the fine sea salt, and 1 teaspoon of the chives. Add the butter and use your fingertips to rub the flour-butter mixture together until a coarse meal forms. Add 3 tablespoons of ice water and stir until the dough just comes together, adding more water by the teaspoonful as needed. Gather into a ball and flatten into a disk. Wrap in plastic or reusable beeswax wrap; chill until firm, at least 1 hour and up to 3 days.

While the dough chills, line a plate or baking sheet with paper towels and place the tomato rounds in a single layer on the paper towels. Sprinkle with the remaining ½ teaspoon of fine sea salt and set aside to drain for at least 45 minutes.

On a lightly floured surface, roll out the chilled dough into an 11-inch [28 cm] circle. Transfer and gently press into a 9-inch [23 cm] tart pan, letting the excess hang over the edges. Use the rolling pin to roll across the top of the pan edges to cut the extra dough cleanly off (reserve the excess dough and bake off separately, see Note). Chill the crust-lined tart pan for at least 15 minutes.

Preheat the oven to 400°F [200°C].

Add the crème fraîche to the chilled crust and spread into a thin, even layer. Season with fine sea salt and black pepper and sprinkle with the remaining 1 teaspoon of chives. Pat the tomato slices dry with paper towels and add to the tart in a single layer. Sprinkle with flaky sea salt and bake until the crust is deeply golden brown and the filling is bubbling and nearly set (it will finish setting as it cools), about 1 hour. Serve at room temperature.

CROQUE MADAME

Makes 6 sandwiches

Béchamel

3 tablespoons unsalted European butter

¼ cup [35 g] all-purpose flour

1½ cups [360 ml] whole milk, warm

3 tablespoons whole-grain mustard

½ teaspoon paprika

Large pinch of freshly grated nutmeg

Fine sea salt

Croque Madame

Twelve ¾-inch [2 cm] slices country bread

12 slices ham, preferably Paris ham

3 cups [240 g] grated Gruyère cheese

½ teaspoon herbes de Provence

Freshly ground black pepper

6 tablespoons [12 g] finely grated Parmigiano-Reggiano

¼ cup [60 ml] extra-virgin olive oil

12 sage leaves

Flaky sea salt

6 large eggs

I ate the worst croque monsieur of my life at a stupidly cute Parisian bistro on the corner of a cobblestoned street in the Marais. The glow of the heat lamps, the quality of the wine and people-watching, and the fact that I was on an otherwise lovely third date did what was possible to save the under-cheesed, under-toasted, under-salted ham and cheese sandwich, but I left craving better. A week later, this croque madame entered my life.

Rich, cheesy, creamy, crunchy, it's an all-around superlative sandwich experience. The female pronoun-ed madame has an egg on top and doesn't shy away from double-decker layers of béchamel. Add a bottle of chilled red, and a Lactaid pill depending on your constitution, and it's an excellent choice for a fourth date.

To make the béchamel: In a medium saucepan over medium heat, add the butter and cook until melted. Whisk in the flour and cook, whisking constantly, until the mixture is lightly browned, about 3 minutes. Slowly pour in the milk, stirring constantly, and cook until the sauce thickens, about 3 minutes more. Remove the pan from the heat and stir in the mustard, paprika, and nutmeg; season with salt.

To make the croque madame: Preheat the oven to 425°F [220°C]. Line a baking sheet with parchment paper.

Spread the béchamel evenly over each slice of bread, making sure to spread all the way to the edges. Place six of the slices, béchamel-side up, on the baking sheet. Divide the ham between the six slices and divide half of the Gruyère among them. Sprinkle with half the herbes de Provence and season with pepper. Top with the remaining slices, béchamel-side up, to form six sandwiches. Top with the remaining Gruyère and sprinkle each with 1 tablespoon of the Parmigiano-Reggiano; sprinkle with the remaining herbes de Provence and season with pepper. Transfer to the oven and bake until the cheese is melted and starting to brown, 15 to 20 minutes.

cont'd

Note
Assembled and unbaked sandwiches can be covered and refrigerated up to overnight, a.k.a. throw together the easiest dinner and/or dinner party of your life the following night.

When the sandwiches are nearly finished, fry the sage and eggs. Line a small plate with paper towels. In a large skillet over medium-high heat, add the oil. Once the oil is very hot, add the sage leaves and fry until crisp and translucent, 2 to 3 seconds. Use a fish spatula to transfer to the paper towel–lined plate; sprinkle with flaky salt. Add the eggs to the oil one at a time, making sure to keep space between each, working in batches if needed. Cook the eggs, shaking the pan occasionally, until the edges are golden brown, about 2 minutes. Tilt the pan gently to pool the oil and, using a spoon, spoon the hot oil over the egg whites and continue to cook, about 1 minute more. Use the fish spatula to transfer each to the top of a croque madame, season with salt and pepper, sprinkle with sage leaves, and serve.

RACLETTE, OR CHEESE DINNER WITH CARBS

Serves 6 to 8

3 pounds [1.25 kg] small red, white, or purple new potatoes

3 to 4 pounds [1.4 to 1.8 kg] sliced raclette or other firm, meltable cheese such as Gruyère, Comté, Cantal, or Morbier cheese

1¼ to 2 pounds [570 to 910 g] mixed charcuterie

Cornichons, for serving

Pickled onions, for serving

Olives, for serving

Baguette or crusty bread, for serving

Note

I live in an apartment devoid of excess storage, so I'm no fan of any extraneous kitchen tools that are pulled out a few times a year at best. That said, I own a raclette grill. Some recipes I've seen say, "Use your broiler!" And, sure, you could, but that breaks the joy of staying tucked around the table, bumping elbows and playing footsie and pouring more wine. You can find them for a fair price, and the experience of gathering to be cozy and overeat cheese on carbs is well worth making a little space in a cabinet (or under a bed!) during the off-season.

From the moment the weather hints at winter right through spring equinox, someone in France is hosting a raclette party. Taken from the French word "racler," which means to scrape, "raclette" refers to both the highly meltable Alpine cheese and the dish itself. It has medieval origins—shepherds in the Middle Ages would use a hot stone to melt the cut side of a half wheel of cheese, scraping the melted portion over cooked potatoes. Regardless of what more modern recipes tell you, every French person in my life insists that raclette should remain a simple affair: sliced cheese, boiled potatoes, and some cold cuts, cornichons, and pickled onions. Add a jar of mustard, some olives, a salad, and crusty bread to the table, but keep any extraneous vegetables for whatever redemptive lunch you have planned the next day—the name of this particular game is cheese, with carbs. Speaking of, if your friends—French or otherwise—are anything like mine, make sure you buy around 8 ounces [230 g] of cheese per person when hosting a raclette party. Honestly, maybe more.

In a large pot, add the potatoes and fill with enough cold water to come 2 inches [5 cm] over the top of the potatoes. Bring to a boil over high heat, then lower the heat to a simmer and cook until the potatoes are tender, 15 to 20 minutes. Drain in a colander and transfer to a serving platter.

Place a raclette grill (see Note) in the center of the table. Arrange the cheese, charcuterie, cornichons, onions, and olives on dishes around the grill. Let guests build their own by placing slices of cheese (and maybe a potato or two) on their individual trays and broiling under the raclette grill until the cheese melts and starts to brown at the edges. Since it takes 5 minutes or so for the cheese to properly cook, encourage guests to put a new slice under as soon as they've scraped the former onto their plate.

GREEN SHAKSHUKA

Serves 6 to 8

2 large bunches green Swiss chard, leaves torn and stems finely chopped

6 cups [120 g] packed baby spinach

1 bunch fresh cilantro, leaves picked

1 bunch fresh flat-leaf parsley, leaves picked

1 jalapeño, stemmed and seeded (optional)

¾ teaspoon ground cumin

8 tablespoons [120 ml] extra-virgin olive oil

Fine sea salt

Freshly ground black pepper

2 large leeks, tough outer layer and dark tops removed, halved, cleaned, and thinly sliced

2 garlic cloves, finely chopped

1 lemon, juiced

6 to 8 large eggs

¼ cup [5 g] dill, coarsely chopped

Crème fraîche, for serving

Crusty bread, for serving

When you move to a new country, don't speak the language, identify fully as an introvert, and work from home, finding places that learn both your coffee order and your name matter. Café Oberkampf in the 11ème was—and still is—that place for me. They also have this herby, green shakshuka that—coming from Los Angeles to a city that doesn't often prioritize healthy green things—feels a little like home too. Here's my take.

Prepare an ice bath in a large bowl and set aside. Bring a large pot of salted water to a boil. Working in batches, add the chard leaves and spinach and blanch for 10 seconds. Use a slotted spoon to transfer the leaves to the prepared ice bath and cool completely. Drain and use your hands to squeeze out excess water. Add the blanched leaves to a food processor or blender along with three-quarters of the cilantro, the parsley, jalapeño (if using), cumin, and 5 tablespoons [80 ml] of the oil. Season with salt and pepper and blend until smooth.

Preheat the oven to 350°F [180°C].

In a large ovenproof skillet over medium heat, add the remaining 3 tablespoons of oil. Once the oil is hot, add the leeks and chard stems and cook, stirring occasionally, until they are soft, 10 to 15 minutes. Add the garlic and cook until soft, about 3 minutes. Stir in the chard purée and lemon juice and season with salt and pepper. Use the back of a wooden spoon to create six to eight shallow divots and crack an egg into each. Season with salt. Bake until the egg whites are just set, 18 to 23 minutes.

Serve with the remaining cilantro, the dill, crème fraîche, and crusty bread.

FRENCH ONION SOUP WITH COGNAC

Serves 6

¼ cup [60 ml] extra-virgin olive oil

1 large head garlic, halved crosswise

4 pounds [1.8 kg] yellow onions (6 to 8 medium), thinly sliced

Fine sea salt

Freshly ground black pepper

½ cup [120 ml] cognac or Armagnac

1 tablespoon apple cider vinegar

10 cups [2.4 L] vegetable stock, store-bought or homemade (see Note)

1 bay leaf

Six to eight ½-inch [12 mm] slices country bread

12 to 16 slices Comté or Gruyère cheese

Note

Store-bought stock isn't really a thing in France. But even if you're using store-bought, bolster the flavor by starting with that instead of water. In a large pot or Dutch oven, combine 12 cups [2.8 L] of water with a few of the onion peels, another bay leaf, some peppercorns, and any vegetable scraps you have lying around and simmer until it reduces to 8 cups [2 L]. Strain and use as the recipe suggests.

Every time I've eaten or made French onion soup, it's . . . decadent: rich beef stock, a good dose of butter, plus the requisite bubbling cover of melted cheese. Then one cold, dark-at-4-p.m. Parisian winter day, I invited friends for dinner and included a vegan in the mix (she's French and her mother cried when she told her). So I adapted, using olive oil instead of butter and aromatic vegetable stock rather than beef stock, and compensated for the dual loss of richness with an entire head of garlic, cognac, and an extra-long cook time. We left the cheese off her bowl and shared the extra slices among the rest of us. The final result is, for me, better than the original and a new go-to.

Heat the oil in a large Dutch oven or pot over medium heat. Add the garlic halves, cut-side down, and cook until golden brown, 3 to 4 minutes. Remove the garlic halves and reserve. Add the onions to the pot, season with salt and pepper, and cook, stirring occasionally at the beginning and more frequently as you near the end, until the onions are deeply golden brown, about 1 hour and 15 minutes.

Add the cognac and vinegar to the onions and use a wooden spoon to scrape up the browned bits from the bottom of the pot. Cook until the liquid is nearly reduced, about 3 minutes; add the vegetable stock, reserved garlic halves, and the bay leaf and bring the mixture to a boil. Lower the heat and simmer, stirring occasionally, until the liquid is reduced by one-third and the onions are extremely tender, about 1 hour. Remove the garlic halves (you can eat the cloves!) and bay leaf. Season with salt and pepper.

Preheat the broiler. Divide the soup among heat-proof bowls and place on a baking sheet. Cut the country bread pieces slightly bigger than the bowls and gently tuck them into the bowls. Top each with two slices of cheese. Broil until the cheese is melted and golden brown in spots, 3 to 8 minutes depending on the strength of your broiler. Serve hot.

SOUP À LA PERSILLADE

Serves 6

1 cup [160 g] dried white beans such as cannellini or navy, picked over, soaked overnight, and drained

1 cup [160 g] dried kidney or cranberry beans, soaked overnight and drained

1 bay leaf

4 garlic cloves, smashed

2 medium yellow onions

6 tablespoons [90 ml] extra-virgin olive oil

Fine sea salt

4 medium carrots, diced

2 medium fennel bulbs, diced

1 medium leek, tough outer layer and dark tops removed, halved, cleaned, and sliced into thin half-moons

1 head Swiss chard, leaves torn and stems finely chopped

Freshly ground black pepper

One 15-ounce [430 g] can chopped tomatoes

Pinch of red pepper flakes

6 cups [1.4 L] vegetable stock, store-bought or homemade (see Note, page 177)

¾ cup [85 g] small shell pasta

½ cup [120 g] Persillade (page 74)

Soup au pistou is a classic Provençal vegetable soup made in the summer when basil and fresh shelling beans are plentiful. Soup à la persillade is for the rest of the year when you're not in Provence and haven't seen the sun in what feels like months. Persillade, a parsley and garlic–forward spread also from Provence, takes the place of the pistou (basically a basil pesto without the pine nuts). I use a mix of heartier veg such as fennel and chard, but use whatever is at your market, in season, and/or sounds delicious to you. Purists will tell you that soup au pistou should be made with water, not stock, but as discussed, this is soup à la persillade, so go wild.

In a large saucepan over medium-high heat, add the drained beans, bay leaf, two of the garlic cloves, half an onion, 3 tablespoons of the oil, and enough water to come 3 inches [7.5 cm] above the top of the beans. Bring to a simmer, then lower the heat to low and cook until the beans are tender, 1 to 1½ hours. Discard the onion half, bay leaf, and garlic cloves, season with salt, and set aside.

Meanwhile, in a large soup pot or Dutch oven over medium heat, heat the remaining 3 tablespoons of oil. Dice the remaining 1½ onions and add to the pot along with the carrots, fennel, leek, and chopped chard stems. Season with salt and pepper and cook, stirring occasionally, until the vegetables are tender, 15 to 20 minutes. Finely chop the remaining two garlic cloves and add to the onion mixture. Cook for 2 minutes, then stir in the tomatoes and red pepper flakes and continue to cook for 5 minutes. Add the beans and their cooking liquid as well as the vegetable stock and bring to a boil. Lower the heat to a simmer and add the pasta and Swiss chard leaves. Cook until the pasta is al dente, about 10 minutes.

Season with salt and pepper and ladle into bowls. Serve hot with the persillade on the table for each guest to stir in.

DINNER PARTY TIPS, DEBUNKED

Google "dinner party tips" and you'll come up with a lot of lists that tend toward the way our parents and grandparents and Emily Post entertained. It's not surprising—these rules have been on magazine stands and in our heads for decades. Sure, there's a few that stand the test of time, but many, like those below, should be retired, posthaste.

Assigned Seating

If you want que la moutarde me monte au nez (literally, "to put the mustard up my nose" but French for "me to lose my temper"), assign me a seat at dinner. I can't tell you how many times I've read that it's proper to "separate couples and close friends," "alternate men and women," and "station the host(s) at opposite ends of the table." All bullshit, here's why:

"ALTERNATE MEN AND WOMEN"

Gender is a construct and alternating seating arrangements by the binary is deductive, assumptive, and honestly, stupid for a lot of reasons. Be better.

"STATION THE HOST(S) AT OPPOSITE ENDS OF THE TABLE"

Unless the end of the table is also closest to the kitchen, I don't care if I sit there. The only thing I prefer when seating myself as host is a spot that allows me easy access to get up without disturbing others so I can grab more wine, water, food, or dessert, or a towel when something spills.

"SEPARATE COUPLES AND CLOSE FRIENDS"

People come to a gathering to spend time with people they know and love, yes, even if they see each other all the time. It's nice to be with people you like, and it's nice to be trusted to sit in a formation that suits. It also offers a sense of security, especially for those of us with social anxiety. If you want to sit next to your partner, friend, crush, ex-lover, go for it! If you don't, don't! We're all grown-ups capable of making decisions for our own bodies ourselves. And if you *do* want me to tell you where to sit, I will, and my answer will probably be "right here next to me" with direct eye contact, a smile, and a quick handhold because you sound a little uncomfortable for whatever reason and I got you.

On the related topic of place cards

My table in Paris is a big slab of marble that comfortably seats six, eight if you get creative, or ten if everyone mutually and consensually gives up any notion of personal space. No matter where you're sitting, you can talk to or reach out and pass a dish or wine to anyone else. If the group or table is larger than this or if it's a special occasion and I'm feeling crafty (see "A Smaller Remarque," following), I can get on board with a simple, beautiful place card setup. That said, they're sheets of paper with names on them and nothing is nailed down, so I make sure to let guests know that the place cards are a visually appealing rough sketch to keep things organized rather than a mandate. If you'd rather sit next to your crush, far be it from me, your humble host, to interfere.

A SMALLER REMARQUE ON FEELING CRAFTY

For how unfussy I like my gatherings to be, there's sometimes reason to fuss: a birthday, a new job, the end of a terrible job, a breakup, and completing the process of freezing your eggs are a few good examples. One of my favorite ways to create a special space for someone I love without a trip to Party City is to take a permanent marker, write up the night's menu on an old poster or big piece of craft paper, and temporarily stick it on the wall. There have been multiple times when that oversized menu has gone home with the honored guest. Proof that you don't need to spend a lot of money or time or, honestly, even have a particularly artistic eye to show someone you support them.

Formulaic To-Do Lists

Don't get me wrong, I love and use to-do lists all the time for all reasons, but let's stop it already with the all-purpose, step-by-step, micromanaged dinner party time lines that start two weeks in advance and end ten minutes after the party starts. Every person and party is different, and also, who is sending out paper invites weeks in advance? Hosting a gathering can and should be enjoyable—relaxing even—no matter if you've done it once a week for the last year or it's your first time ever (go you!). Instead of following some time line written for the masses, make your own (that is, if you're a list person. If you're not, do whatever keeps you relaxed and on track).

That's not to say I'm not *all for* pre-dinner planning, especially if you're solo-hosting and have the rest of your life to work in around your evening. One way I do this is to grab all the plates, platters, small dishes, glasses, silverware, and serving utensils (namely, anything that's going on the final table) and bring them out to the table earlier in the day. I jot a quick note on a Post-it or scrap of paper to remind myself what's going on which serving dish, from mains and sides to that small dish that will eventually be full of olive pits. That way, (a) you know everything fits, and (b) if someone offers to set the table or you're feeling harried, it's already thought out.

If I'm making a bigger meal or have other stuff to do the day of the gathering, I also try to shop for as many items as I can a day or two early so I'm not feeling stressed and sweaty before I even get in the kitchen.

Start-Time Shaming

I'm an on-time person. If you tell me to show up somewhere at 7 p.m., I'm there with a red lip on and walking around the block at 6:50 p.m. So I take personal offense to any nitpicking "tip" that disparages guests for arriving anything but fashionably late. *That said*, I live in France, where start times are truly a suggestion and friends often show up an hour after the time I texted. If your guests are on time and you're still getting things ready or have yet to shower, please don't shame them for showing up when you told them to. Reminder: You like them! Instead, greet timely guests at the door, offer them a drink and a snack and possibly some herbs to pick if you're in the weeds. If your guests are late, greet them at the door, offer them a drink and a snack and remember that they might be running behind for a variety of reasons like work or a call with their mom or a fight with their partner or the Métro was delayed (one exception and this is hyper-specialized, but my LA people: I'm sorry but you can't use traffic as an excuse anymore—we all know when to leave if you have a dinner during rush hour). Regardless of the reason, if someone comes in nearly an hour after your first guests arrived, they're coming in at the end of apéro hour and they too deserve something special to open the night.

Lastly

This isn't so much a debunking as it is a strong personal belief. Four things should be on every French (or not) table so guests never have to ask for them: salt, pepper, butter, and water. Who cares if you seasoned that steak perfectly or you know people will fill up on bread and butter? They're individuals with individual tastes and preferences and bodies, and asking for salt always feels super rude, and if you're my friends Alexis and Akira, you like to eat big flakes of Maldon as your pre- and post-dessert snack. Also, hydration is important to life itself, so try to have water available at all times.

SIDES

Salade Verte with Cornichon Vinaigrette | page 210

CARROTS WITH PIMENT D'ESPELETTE

Serves 4 to 6

3 pounds [1.4 kg] carrots, cleaned and trimmed

4 fresh thyme sprigs

3 tablespoons extra-virgin olive oil

1 teaspoon piment d'Espelette

2 teaspoons fine sea salt

1½ tablespoons unsalted European butter

Note
Other recipes to test your potential new partner's tolerance for (mild) spice are Pipérade Dip (page 77), Socca + Parm (page 86), and Basque Chicken (page 116).

Dating in France is often like dating in many places, from what I can tell, but sometimes with the Eiffel Tower in view. It's generally depressing, but it's also just enough to (usually) keep you coming back. For some—for me—there is lots of wine. There are, however, some cultural differences. While I could go into the stereotypical (but no less true in my experience) tête-à-tête between American-born optimism and deeply rooted French pessimism or how the level of passion one might expect from a French partner often corresponds to the amount of drama in the relationship, there's one difference that truly blindsided me: The French aren't known for their tolerance of spice. While this may not be a deal breaker for some, you know it is for me if you've ever seen me with my peppermill. That said, I'm keeping the faith because piment d'Espelette, a French pepper from the Basque region of France, is sweet, smoky, rich, and only mildly hot. I use it heartily but especially so when I'm getting to know someone new and cute.

Preheat the oven to 450°F [230°C].

On a large baking sheet, combine the carrots, thyme, oil, and piment d'Espelette. Season with the salt and toss to coat. Dot with the butter and roast, tossing occasionally, until very tender and browned, 35 to 40 minutes. Serve hot or at room temperature.

PARSNIPS WITH FENNEL + HONEYCOMB

Serves 6

1½ pounds [680 g] parsnips, trimmed and halved lengthwise (quartered if large)

2 medium fennel bulbs, trimmed, halved lengthwise, and cut into ¼-inch [6 mm] slices, fronds reserved

2 garlic cloves, unpeeled and lightly smashed

¼ cup [60 ml] extra-virgin olive oil

Fine sea salt

Ground white pepper

3 tablespoons dry white wine

½ cup [70 g] pitted black olives

2 ounces [55 g] honeycomb, cut into small pieces

Flaky sea salt

Honeycomb is made of edible wax, meaning it's ready to eat—from the chewy comb to the encased rich liquid honey—and offers a range of textures along the way. The experience is especially satisfying when paired with soft roasted parsnips and fennel. If you can't find honeycomb, drizzle the finished dish with a liquid honey; if you can, buy extra and use it on your next cheese plate (see page 273).

Preheat the oven to 400°F [200°C].

On a large baking sheet, combine the parsnips, fennel, and garlic. Drizzle with the oil and season with salt and white pepper. Roast until the parsnips and fennel are golden and very tender, tossing halfway through, about 40 minutes total.

Remove the sheet from the oven and add the wine. Use a wooden spoon to scrape up any browned bits from the bottom of the sheet. Remove the roasted garlic, allow to cool slightly, then peel and smash into a paste. Return the garlic paste to the pan and use your hands to gently massage the garlic into the vegetables. Transfer to a serving platter and scatter the olives and honeycomb pieces over the top. Sprinkle with the reserved fennel fronds and season with flaky salt. Serve immediately.

ROASTED NECTARINES + SHALLOTS

Serves 4 to 6

¼ cup [60 ml] extra-virgin olive oil

2 tablespoons red wine vinegar

1 teaspoon grainy mustard

20 shallots, peeled and halved (large shallots quartered)

Fine sea salt

Freshly ground black pepper

6 ripe nectarines, quartered and pitted

When I first moved to Paris, I enrolled in French lessons at a school in the 11ème. I did so well on my initial written evaluation that they placed me in an advanced level and, while a continued disparity between my written and verbal French has come in handy during my visa process, this humble brag stops here. There are few things more sobering than a boost of confiance ("confidence") immediately followed by a walk of shame across the hall to the beginners' class. I would like you to know, however, that I'm proof that the French phrase for blushing—rouge comme une tomate (literally "red like a tomato")—is extremely accurate.

On Tuesdays and Fridays, I would temper my broken ego with as many ripe nectarines as I could carry from the red-and-white-striped fruit stand at the outdoor market down the block (and a glass of rosé at a nearby wine bar). Years later, my spoken French still lags behind my written, the nectarine stall at the Marché Popincourt is still there, and while I no longer go to that little school, my therapist is on the same street, and I insist on seeing her on Tuesdays or Fridays.

Preheat the oven to 400°F [200°F].

In a small bowl, whisk together the oil, vinegar, and mustard. Scatter the shallots on a baking sheet and pour the oil-vinegar mixture over the top. Toss to coat and season with salt and pepper. Roast for 20 minutes, then remove the pan from the heat and add the nectarines. Toss to coat with a spatula and season again with salt and pepper. Roast until the shallots and nectarines are very tender, 15 to 20 minutes more. Serve warm or at room temperature.

HARICOTS VERTS WITH TAPENADE

Serves 4 to 6

1½ pounds [680 g] haricots verts or green beans, trimmed

¼ cup [75 g] black olive tapenade

2 tablespoons extra-virgin olive oil

Fine sea salt

Freshly ground black pepper

¼ cup [10 g] finely chopped flat-leaf parsley

Go to a farmers' market in the south of France in August and you'll find two things: a large percentage of Parisians escaping the heat waves, and tapenade. So. Much. Tapenade. This recipe combines said olive spread with another excellent item you'll find plenty of at most late-summer marchés, French or otherwise: green beans. Best of all, you need access only to a pot of boiling water and a large serving bowl to make this—no relying on dull rental kitchen IKEA knives.

Bring a large pot of salted water to a boil. Add the haricots verts and cook until bright green and crisp-tender, 4 to 5 minutes.

While the beans cook, whisk together the tapenade and oil in a large serving bowl. Drain the beans and transfer to the bowl. Toss to coat, season with salt and pepper, and finish with parsley. Serve warm or at room temperature.

TOMATES OUBLIÉES

Serves 4 to 6

8 cups [1.3 kg] cherry tomatoes

1 small head garlic, halved lengthwise

½ cup [120 ml] extra-virgin olive oil

½ cup [120 ml] dry vermouth

4 fresh rosemary sprigs

4 fresh thyme sprigs

Fine sea salt

Translated to "forgotten tomatoes," that's exactly what you should do with these after you put them in the oven. Three hours later when your timer goes off they'll be a very soft, very sweet, very good thing to put alongside your meal or alongside a fresh cheese or alongside nothing because a small, perfect thing is enough most days. Points for doing this during tomato season, but in case you're in a different season, don't skip over to a carrot dish just yet—the long, slow bake returns even the least interesting out-of-season tomato to its sweet potential.

Preheat the oven to 225°F [110°C].

On a baking sheet, combine the tomatoes, garlic halves, oil, vermouth, rosemary, and thyme. Season generously with salt and toss to coat. Make sure the garlic halves are cut-side down and place the sheet in the oven until the cherry tomatoes and garlic cloves are very soft, 3 hours. Serve warm or at room temperature.

TOMATOES WITH BUTTER + ARMAGNAC

Serves 6

3 tablespoons Armagnac

2 tablespoons unsalted European butter, melted and cooled slightly

1 medium shallot, finely chopped

Fine sea salt

Freshly ground black pepper

4 large heirloom tomatoes, cut into large pieces

1½ tablespoons finely chopped fresh chives

Flaky sea salt

Some would say it's sacrilege to cover a perfectly ripe tomato with anything. They clearly haven't covered a perfectly ripe tomato with butter and Armagnac. The combination is rich and refreshing, lightly boozy and acidic, and, bonus, it sets you up to keep the bottle of the French brandy casually on the table all the way through your meal.

In a small dish, combine the Armagnac, butter, and shallot. Season with fine sea salt and pepper. Set aside for 10 minutes. Arrange the tomatoes on a large platter, drizzle with the Armagnac-shallot mixture, and sprinkle with the chives and flaky salt. Serve immediately.

EGGPLANT CONFIT

Serves 4 to 6

One 1-pound [455 g] eggplant

Fine sea salt

3 garlic cloves, thinly sliced

3 anchovy fillets

3 fresh thyme sprigs

1½ cups [360 ml] extra-virgin olive oil

½ teaspoon freshly ground black pepper

As a kid growing up in Wisconsin, my childhood summers meant weekends "up north" to a family cabin in lake country. There I spent countless hours of my young, only-child life wrapped in a life jacket on a pontoon boat in the middle of a lake, staring at a hazy shoreline and pretending that the blurry expanse across the way was Europe and that I was a chic, important woman in the middle of the ocean headed east. As an adult living in France, my summers now mean at least some time in the south. (Absolutely wild to me, still.) This recipe was written there, a bit inland from the seaside, in Provence— land of rosé, olive oil, and insane summer produce that you can't not buy too much of and thus need to find a way to keep the excess. Confit is one of these ways. Just as special as the silky, oil-preserved slices of eggplant is the infused olive oil they're kept in. Use it to fry eggs or pour it on a bunch of other summer produce. You're living the dream, kid.

Preheat the oven to 275°F [135°C]. Line a baking sheet with paper towels.

Trim the top and end of the eggplant, then slice lengthwise into ¾-inch [2 cm] pieces. Sprinkle the eggplant pieces liberally with salt and place salted-side down on the paper towels. Sprinkle the other side with salt. Set aside for 30 minutes.

Blot the eggplants dry with paper towels and slice each lengthwise so you have long ¾-inch [2 cm] slices. Transfer to a large baking dish, arranging the eggplant slices in a single layer. Add the garlic, anchovies, and thyme and pour the oil over the top (the eggplant should be almost fully submerged, but it's OK if it's not completely). Sprinkle with the pepper. Bake until the eggplant slices are very soft, 60 to 75 minutes.

Eggplants can be made up to 4 days in advance and stored completely submerged in oil in the refrigerator.

ROASTED YELLOW PEPPERS WITH CORNICHONS + CAPERS

Serves 4 to 6

6 large yellow bell peppers, stemmed, seeded, and quartered

4 garlic cloves, unpeeled and smashed

6 tablespoons [90 ml] extra-virgin olive oil

Fine sea salt

Freshly ground black pepper

¼ cup [60 ml] cornichon pickling liquid

3 tablespoons finely chopped parsley

5 cornichons, coarsely chopped

2 tablespoons salted capers, soaked, rinsed, and drained

Flaky sea salt

For a long while after I moved into my Paris apartment, I had a mini refrigerator. Not in an "extra refrigerator for wine and beer" kind of way or a funny, haha "I have a small refrigerator that's actually fairly normal sized for Europe" but an actual 17.7-by-17.7-by-20-inch [45 by 45 by 50 cm] bar refrigerator tucked in a cabinet in the kitchen that was my actual real-life refrigerator for things like milk and cheese and one time a leg of lamb. I'm proud of every single dinner party I threw during the mini refrigerator era. The day I got my current "big" refrigerator (it's still smaller than all my American friends' refrigerators by a lot), I moved in all the essentials: butter, sparkling wine, and cornichons.

Often my cornichons are whisked into a vinaigrette (page 210) or rémoulade (page 89) or served alongside a croque madame (page 169) or raclette (page 171). But lately both the small pickles and their brine have been making their way into this easy side. I can attest it goes extremely well with whatever size leg of lamb (page 128) you can fit into your refrigerator.

Preheat the oven to 375°F [190°C].

In a shallow baking dish, add the bell peppers, skin-side down, and the garlic. Drizzle with 2 tablespoons of the oil and season with salt and pepper. Bake until the peppers and garlic are very tender and slightly charred around the edges, 35 to 45 minutes. Drizzle with the cornichon pickling liquid and let cool. Peel and finely chop the roasted garlic. Return them to the dish with the peppers and drizzle with 2 tablespoons of the oil. Add 2 tablespoons of the chopped parsley and toss to coat.

Arrange the bell peppers on a serving platter and drizzle the pan sauce over the top. Top with the cornichons, capers, and the remaining 1 tablespoon of parsley. Drizzle with the remaining 2 tablespoons of oil and season with pepper and flaky salt. Serve warm or at room temperature.

(ROASTED) RADISHES WITH BUTTER

Serves 6

2 large bunches radishes, trimmed

3 tablespoons salted or unsalted European butter, cut into small pieces

Freshly ground black pepper

4 cups [80 g] arugula

1 lemon

Flaky sea salt

One of my favorite words you don't learn in French class but you'll pick up the moment you start eavesdropping anywhere in France is "bref." Translated it means "briefly" or "in short," and it is used when someone tries to cut through a long story and get straight to the most important point. Bref, this recipe takes the classic French combination of radishes and butter and roasts the veg. Adding arugula at the end—just long enough to wilt the leaves—takes it from petit snack to full-blown side. Or lunch or dinner for one.

Preheat the oven to 400°F [200°C].

Halve any large radishes. Scatter on a baking sheet and dot with the butter pieces. Season with pepper and roast until the radishes are tender, 15 to 20 minutes.

Remove the pan from the oven and add the arugula. Squeeze the lemon over the top, season with flaky salt and pepper, and toss just until the greens are wilted. Serve warm.

LÉGUMES FARCIS

Serves 6

2 large tomatoes

2 small zucchini, halved lengthwise

1 small eggplant, halved lengthwise

6 tablespoons [90 ml] extra-virgin olive oil, plus more to finish

2 medium shallots, finely chopped

4 garlic cloves, finely chopped

3 anchovies, finely chopped

Fine sea salt

Freshly ground black pepper

½ teaspoon red pepper flakes

2 tablespoons red wine vinegar

2 cups [280 g] finely ground bread crumbs

2 tablespoons finely chopped mint

Flaky sea salt

I first fell in love with this style of baked stuffed vegetables (called either légumes farcis or petits farcis in French) at the Saturday market in Arles. I was shopping hungry when I fixated on a perfectly red, round, overwhelmed-with-stuffing tomato. I very nearly knocked over all the wooden boxes full of peaches and the old ladies jostling for the good ones at the stall alongside to get to it. Stuffed with sausage, herbs, and bread crumbs and eaten in big, messy bites, it kept me from assaulting anyone.

The version I make at home uses a mix of vegetables and skips the sausage, letting the legumes shine and thus making it an excellent side for meaty and not-meaty mains alike. If you're not big on anchovies—or vegan—you could leave them out (just add a little more oil and salt), but I don't recommend it if all else is equal.

Cut the tops off the tomatoes and use a spoon to scrape out the insides, reserving the pulp in a small bowl and leaving a thick-enough outer wall to keep the tomato intact. Use a spoon to scrape out the insides of the zucchini and eggplant, leaving a ¼-inch [6 mm] outer wall. Finely chop the zucchini and eggplant insides and reserve.

In a large skillet over medium heat, add 3 tablespoons of the oil. Once the oil is hot, add the shallots and cook until tender, 5 to 7 minutes. Add the garlic and anchovies and cook for another minute. Add 1 tablespoon of the oil to the pan, then add the chopped zucchini and eggplant and season with salt and pepper. Cook, stirring occasionally, until the liquid released from the vegetables is almost evaporated, about 7 minutes. Stir in the tomato pulp and red pepper flakes and cook until the liquid is almost evaporated, about 10 minutes. Pour in the vinegar and cook for 1 minute. Season with salt and pepper. Stir in the bread crumbs and chopped mint.

Preheat the oven to 375°F [190°C].

Arrange the scooped-out vegetables on a baking sheet or large baking dish, cut-sides up. Season the insides with salt and pepper, then spoon the vegetable–bread crumb mixture into the vegetables, mounding it slightly. Drizzle with the remaining 2 tablespoons of oil and sprinkle with flaky sea salt. Bake until the vegetables are tender, about 30 minutes. Serve warm or at room temperature, drizzled with more oil if desired.

RED KURI SQUASH WITH CIDER + SAUCISSON

Serves 4 to 6

2 tablespoons extra-virgin olive oil

1 large shallot, thinly sliced into rounds

1 red Fresno chile, seeded and thinly sliced

Fine sea salt

Ground white pepper

2 tablespoons apple cider vinegar

1½ cups [360 ml] dry hard cider, preferably from Normandy

2 small red kuri squash, seeded and cut into ¾-inch [2 cm] wedges

2 ounces [55 g] saucisson, thinly sliced (about 20 slices)

Note
Speaking from experience, leftover squash + cornichons + Cheddar + mustard on rye is an ideal sandwich to bring to the beach or near a warm fire, depending on where in the world you spend squash season.

Red kuri (or Hokkaido, or potimarron in French) is the queen of squash. The teardrop-shaped, red-orange squash has edible skin (in general, the smaller the squash, the more tender the skin) and a flavor that could be described as a less-sweet sweet potato mixed with a chestnut. Braising it in dry hard cider laced with chiles and shallots brings out its sweetness. Bonus: The dish is vegan all the way up to the final saucisson add, if you or one of your guests is into that sort of thing.

Set a large Dutch oven or large, deep skillet over medium heat and add the oil. Once the oil is hot, add the shallot and chile and season with salt and white pepper. Cook, stirring, for 3 minutes. Stir in the vinegar and cook until nearly evaporated, about 1 minute. Add the cider and squash and bring to a boil. Cover and cook, turning the squash slices occasionally, until the squash is very tender, 20 to 25 minutes. Season with salt and white pepper.

Add the saucisson slices to the squash and toss to coat with the sauce and heat through. Serve warm.

LAZY DUX

Serves 6

3 tablespoons extra-virgin olive oil

3 tablespoons unsalted European butter

2 medium shallots, thinly sliced

2 garlic cloves, finely chopped

2 pounds [910 g] wild mushrooms, such as creminis, porcini, and/or shiitakes, quartered

Fine sea salt

Freshly ground black pepper

1 tablespoon dry vermouth

The difference between Lazy Dux and classic French duxelles lies in the amount of chopping required. Lazy though it may be, it's also a flavorful side that feels fancy yet requires little more than nominal knife skills and access to good butter. Mince everything much smaller, and you have a recipe for classic mushroom duxelles, used in things like beef Wellington and also served on toast points, but don't be a show-off—we're going for maximum approachability here.

In a large skillet over medium heat, add the oil and butter and heat until the butter is melted. Add the shallots and garlic and cook until the shallot softens, 3 to 5 minutes. Add the mushrooms and cook until they are tender and browned, 15 to 20 minutes. Season with salt and pepper. Pour in the vermouth and use a wooden spoon to scrape up any brown bits off the bottom of the skillet. Continue to cook until the vermouth and any liquid released from the mushrooms evaporates, 2 to 5 minutes more. Serve warm.

GREENS WITH ROASTED TOMATO VINAIGRETTE

Serves 4 to 6

3 cups [480 g] cherry tomatoes

2 garlic cloves, finely chopped

6 tablespoons [90 ml] extra-virgin olive oil

1 tablespoon honey

2 tablespoons finely chopped mint leaves

½ teaspoon Dijon mustard

Fine sea salt

Freshly ground black pepper

1 large head leafy greens

The first dinner party I threw in France was in August, also known to France as the month every restaurant, bar, and café in Paris closes for vacance and to the rest of the Northern Hemisphere as tomato season. Roasting the tomatoes with garlic and honey brings out even more sweetness, and as they burst in the oven the juices create a stupidly good base for vinaigrette that should be in your regular rotation.

Preheat the oven to 400°F [200°C].

In a medium baking dish, combine the tomatoes, garlic, 3 tablespoons of the oil, the honey, and 1 tablespoon of the mint. Roast until the tomatoes are very soft and begin to burst, about 30 minutes. Set aside to cool.

Use a slotted spoon to transfer the tomatoes to a plate. Use a spatula to scrape the liquid from the baking dish into a large bowl. Whisk in the mustard. Whisking constantly, add the remaining 3 tablespoons of oil in a steady stream until emulsified. Season with salt and pepper and stir in the remaining 1 tablespoon of mint. Add the greens and reserved tomatoes to the bowl and toss gently to coat. Serve immediately.

SUCRINE WEDGE

Serves 6

1 small shallot, finely chopped

1 tablespoon red wine vinegar

1 lemon, juiced

Fine sea salt

Freshly ground black pepper

3 tablespoons crème fraîche

2 tablespoons heavy cream

1 cup [120 g] crumbled blue cheese

4 ounces [115 g] lardons or bacon, cut crosswise into ¼-inch [6 mm] strips

6 to 8 heads sucrine lettuce, quartered

3 radishes, thinly sliced into rounds

Note
If you can't find sucrine lettuce, look for Little Gem or use a mix of romaine hearts and butter (Boston) lettuce.

Keep your B.E.C., your Bloody Mary, your Pedialyte—when I'm hung over I make wedge salad. It's rich, creamy, fatty, and *just* fresh enough to feel as if I'm nourishing what life is left of my wine-coated insides. Sucrine lettuce heads look like small romaine, taste slightly sweet, and deliver an iceberg-like crunch. A very pro move is to serve one big, communal platter of sucrine wedge salad with Party Steak (page 120) and bottles of red wine, and make sure you have extras of all the salad ingredients for the inevitable day after.

In a small bowl, combine the shallot, vinegar, and lemon juice. Season with salt and pepper and set aside for 15 minutes. Whisk in the crème fraîche and heavy cream, then crumble in ½ cup [60 g] of the blue cheese and stir to combine. Set aside.

Line a small plate with paper towels. In a small skillet over medium heat, add the lardons and cook until browned and crisp, 5 to 7 minutes. Transfer to the paper towel–lined plate.

On a platter, arrange the lettuce quarters and top with the radish rounds, lardons, and the remaining ½ cup [60 g] of blue cheese. Drizzle with the prepared dressing and season with pepper. Serve immediately.

SALADE VERTE WITH CORNICHON VINAIGRETTE

Serves 4 to 6

Cornichon Vinaigrette

6 cornichons, thinly sliced

1 medium shallot, thinly sliced into rounds

3 tablespoons fresh lemon juice

2 tablespoons cornichon pickling liquid

1 teaspoon Dijon mustard

1 teaspoon honey

Fine sea salt

Freshly ground black pepper

¼ cup [60 ml] extra-virgin olive oil

Salade Verte

1 large head leafy greens, torn

Note

At any time during the day of your dinner, add the cornichon vinaigrette (or whatever dressing you're using) to the bottom of a salad bowl and layer cleaned and dried greens on top. Store in the refrigerator until you're ready for dinner, then toss and serve.

One of my favorite marchés in France is the night market in the Provençal town of Velleron. It's a true locals' market, nary a lavender soap stand in sight. Nearly all the vegetables are harvested the day they're sold—my last visit during peak tomato season happily ruined all other tomatoes for me for life. But the real reason it's my favorite is because it's where M. Elie Barthélémy sells his cornichons. He started making them when he was fifteen years old and has spent the past fifty-some-odd years perfecting the crunchy, vinegary apex of small pickles. This salad (pictured on page 185) is an homage to his craft, and if you're ever in the area, please, bring me back a jar.

To make the vinaigrette: In a resealable jar, combine the cornichons, shallot, lemon juice, pickling liquid, mustard, and honey. Season with salt and pepper, stir to combine, and let sit for at least 15 minutes. Pour in the oil, cover the jar tightly with a lid, and shake to emulsify. Season with salt and pepper.

To make the salad: Transfer the dressing to a large salad bowl. Add the greens and toss to coat. Serve immediately.

PARSLEY SALAD

Serves 4

1 large shallot, finely chopped

1 garlic clove, grated on a Microplane

2 tablespoons red wine vinegar

2 tablespoons freshly squeezed grapefruit juice

1½ teaspoons whole-grain mustard

½ teaspoon light honey, such as Acacia

Fine sea salt

Freshly ground black pepper

1 large egg

3 tablespoons extra-virgin olive oil

2 bunches fresh flat-leaf parsley, leaves picked

Thursdays and Sundays are default favorite days of the week in Paris because that's when the Marché Bastille is open. There you'll find row after row of produce, flowers, spinning rotisserie chickens, crêpes, and oyster stalls where you can down a half dozen freshly shucked to order with or without a glass of white wine and no one cares that it's 9 a.m. Although, it's France, where no one ever cares.

But the main reason I love this particular market is because my favorite vegetable vendor is there, rain or shine. With imperfect French on my end and patience on hers, I ask about herbs or greens or a new kind of squash, and while I always walk away with something new, I also always walk away with a few bunches of deeply green, ridiculously fragrant parsley. Parsley this flavorful calls for a simple dressing that's rich but doesn't take over: barely cooked egg, shallot, vinegar, honey, and citrus. If you happen to see a rotisserie chicken at your own market, snag it or make Mayo Roast Chicken (page 115) to serve alongside this salad (pictured on page 114).

In a large bowl, combine the shallot, garlic, vinegar, grapefruit juice, mustard, and honey. Season with salt and pepper and set aside to marinate while you make the egg.

Prepare an ice bath in a bowl and set aside. Bring a small saucepan of salted water to a boil over medium-high heat. Using a slotted spoon, carefully lower the egg into the water. Cook for 5 minutes, adjusting the heat to maintain a gentle boil. Transfer the egg to the ice bath and chill until just slightly warm, about 2 minutes. Use the back of a spoon to gently crack the egg all over and peel. Add it to the shallot mixture and use a fork to smash together. Slowly add the oil, whisking with a fork to emulsify. Season with salt and pepper.

Pile the parsley in a large serving bowl and pour the dressing over the top. Toss to coat, season with salt and pepper, and serve.

ESCAROLE SALAD WITH CONCORD GRAPES

Serves 6

½ cup [120 ml] extra-virgin olive oil

2 shallots, finely chopped

1 garlic clove, grated on a Microplane

2 tablespoons red wine vinegar

1 tablespoon Dijon mustard

Pinch of red pepper flakes

Fine sea salt

Freshly ground black pepper

1 large head escarole, torn into large pieces

8 ounces [230 g] Concord grapes (about 1½ cups)

¾ cup [120 g] green olives, such as Castelvetrano

1 cup [120 g] crumbled blue cheese

This warm, creamy, yet refreshing salad is my go-to the entire length of Concord grape season. Escarole is a member of the chicory family cloaked in the body of a leafy green head of lettuce. It possesses enough bitterness to offset the sweetness of the grapes and the rich cream of the blue cheese, combined with just enough structural integrity to handle a quick sauté. Serve warm and often.

In a large skillet or Dutch oven over medium heat, add the oil. Once the oil is hot, add the shallots and garlic and cook, stirring occasionally, until the shallots are soft and start to caramelize, 7 to 10 minutes. Add the vinegar and cook for 2 minutes, then stir in the mustard and red pepper flakes. Season with salt and black pepper. Turn the heat to low and stir in the escarole. Use a pair of tongs to toss the leaves in the dressing until they start to wilt, then add the grapes, olives, and ½ cup [60 g] of the blue cheese. Stir to combine and melt the cheese, then transfer to a platter and sprinkle with the remaining ½ cup [60 g] of cheese and plenty of black pepper. Serve warm.

EXTREMELY FRENCH CARROT SALAD

Serves 6

3 tablespoons extra-virgin olive oil

3 tablespoons fresh lemon juice

1 teaspoon light honey

½ teaspoon ground cumin

Fine sea salt

1 pound [455 g] carrots, grated on the large holes of a box grater or in a food processor fitted with a grating attachment

½ cup [20 g] coarsely chopped fresh flat-leaf parsley or cilantro

This carrot salad is . . . extremely French. It's also everywhere. You can buy it by the kilo or prepackaged at boucheries and supermarkets and train station kiosks. It's on menus at both classic bistros and the kind of spots you walk into and think you've accidentally touched a portkey to Los Angeles. But it's at its best—and most cost-effective—when made at home. The name in French is carottes râpées, or grated carrots, and that's mostly what it should be: grated raw carrots, lightly dressed with oil and lemon, a bit of cumin, and little else.

In a medium bowl, whisk together the oil, lemon juice, honey, and cumin. Season with salt. Add the carrots and toss to coat, adjusting the dressing to taste. Stir in the parsley and set aside to marinate for at least 30 minutes and up to 2 hours before serving.

CARAMELIZED ENDIVE SALAD

Serves 6

7 tablespoons [105 ml] extra-virgin olive oil

3 tablespoons unsalted European butter

12 medium Belgian endives, halved lengthwise

Fine sea salt

Freshly ground black pepper

1 medium shallot, finely chopped

2 tablespoons heavy cream

1½ tablespoons white wine vinegar

2 teaspoons Dijon mustard

3 tablespoons finely chopped fresh chives

1 garlic clove, halved

⅔ cup [80 g] walnut halves, toasted and coarsely chopped

Endive à la crème is a simple, comforting, classic French dish of endives baked with cream and, often, ham. I love the idea, but the final execution is always too heavy and oddly textured, and to be perfectly honest, if I'm going to eat something baked in cream, why would I choose endive when I can have potatoes? (See page 229.)

This, however, takes the classic's base idea and lightens it into a slightly rich, big-flavored, nicely textured side. Endives are halved, browned in butter, then drizzled with a dressing made with cream, Dijon, and chives. There's no ham in this version, but I can't imagine that a few slices of prosciutto, lightly toasted in the skillet and tucked around the caramelized halves, wouldn't make a welcome addition.

In a large skillet over medium-high heat, add 1½ tablespoons of the oil and 1½ tablespoons of the butter. Once the butter is melted, add half of the endive halves in a single layer, cut-side down. Season with salt and pepper and cook without stirring until the cut sides are lightly brown, about 5 minutes. Use a pair of tongs to turn the endives over, season with salt and pepper, and continue to cook for another 5 minutes. Repeat with 1½ tablespoons of the oil, the remaining 1½ tablespoons of butter, and the remaining endives.

In a medium bowl, whisk together the shallot, heavy cream, vinegar, and mustard. Season with salt and pepper. Whisk in the remaining 4 tablespoons [60 ml] of oil and 1½ tablespoons of the chives.

Rub the inside of a salad bowl with the cut sides of the garlic. Reserve the garlic for another use or discard. Add the warm endive halves and drizzle with the dressing. Toss gently to coat. Sprinkle with the walnuts and the remaining 1½ tablespoons of chives and serve immediately.

LENTIL SALAD WITH PERSILLADE

Serves 6

1½ cups [300 g] French green lentils, preferably lentils du Puy, rinsed and picked through

1 medium shallot, finely chopped

1 bay leaf

Fine sea salt

½ cup [120 g] Persillade (page 74)

2 tablespoons red wine vinegar or white wine vinegar

I admit, this recipe may read a little simple, maybe even boring. It's the thing you reach for when you need a light-ish, healthy-ish side that doubles as a sad desk lunch the next day. *But* simple doesn't equal boring when you coat lentils in a garlicky, parsley-y sauce and a solid douse of vinegar. Make this as far ahead of time as you can to let the lentils soak in the persillade; rejoice at your desk—or dinner table.

In a large saucepan over medium-high heat, combine the lentils, shallot, and bay leaf. Cover with enough water to come 3 to 4 inches [7.5 to 10 cm] above the lentils. Bring to a boil, then season generously with salt and lower the heat to a simmer. Cook until the lentils are just tender, 30 to 35 minutes. Drain through a fine-mesh sieve and transfer the lentils to a medium bowl; discard the bay leaf. Add the persillade and vinegar and stir to combine. Lentils will keep in the refrigerator in a covered container for 4 days.

BUTTERED PEAS + GREENS

Serves 6

3 tablespoons unsalted European butter

1 small shallot, finely chopped

1 tablespoon mild honey

1 small head butter lettuce, leaves thinly sliced

1 pound [455 g] shelled fresh or frozen English peas (about 3¾ cups)

Fine sea salt

Freshly ground black pepper

¼ cup [10 g] finely chopped fresh flat-leaf parsley

3 tablespoons crème fraîche

1 tablespoon fresh lemon juice

Flaky sea salt

Fresh pea season anywhere is a short, glorious moment in time. If you can, make this then. If you can't, know that frozen peas are picked and flash-frozen to tender, sweet perfection at the moment of peak freshness, so whether it's spring in Paris or February in upstate New York, this side is yours for the making.

In a medium saucepan over medium heat, melt the butter. Add the shallot and cook until tender and the butter is starting to brown, 3 to 5 minutes. Add the honey and stir to combine. Stir in the lettuce and peas and season with fine sea salt and pepper. Cover loosely and cook, stirring occasionally, just until the peas are warmed through, 4 to 6 minutes. Stir in the parsley, crème fraîche, and lemon juice and sprinkle with flaky salt. Serve warm.

CARROT TARTE TATIN

Serves 6

4 large carrots, sliced lengthwise into ¼-inch [6 mm] pieces

4 tablespoons [60 ml] extra-virgin olive oil

Fine sea salt

Freshly ground black pepper

2 large leeks, tough outer layer and dark tops removed, halved, cleaned, and sliced into thin half-moons

2 garlic cloves, thinly sliced

2 tablespoons apple cider vinegar

1 tablespoon Dijon mustard

3 tablespoons sugar

4 fresh thyme sprigs

All-purpose flour, for dusting

One 8-ounce [230 g] sheet all-butter puff pastry

I stan a classic apple tarte Tatin, but this carrot version is more versatile and just as delicious. Side? Yep. Main when paired with a big green salad and maybe an on-the-richer-side snack beforehand? Absolutely. Breakfast? I can say from experience, very much yes. Dessert? Probably not, but nothing can be everything to everyone. Two things that make this savory tarte extra special: the hidden layer of leeks bound with Dijon and the generous dusting of black pepper on the puff pastry, resulting in a golden, beautifully spiced final crust.

Preheat the oven to 400°F [200°C].

Arrange the carrot slices in a single layer on a baking sheet and drizzle with 2 tablespoons of the oil. Season with salt and pepper and roast until the carrots are tender, 20 to 25 minutes.

While the carrots roast, heat the remaining 2 tablespoons of oil in a large skillet over medium heat; add the leeks and garlic. Cook, stirring, until the leeks are very tender, about 10 minutes. Add 1 tablespoon of the vinegar and use a wooden spoon to scrape up any brown bits on the bottom of the skillet. Remove the skillet from the heat, stir in the mustard, and set aside. Remove the roasted carrots from the oven and set aside until cool.

In a 9-inch [23 cm] round cake pan or cast-iron skillet over medium heat, add the sugar and 3 tablespoons of water. Cook without stirring until the caramel is deep golden brown, then add the remaining 1 tablespoon of vinegar and the thyme. Remove from the heat and carefully add the carrot slices in a single layer to the pan. Top evenly with the cooled leek mixture.

Lightly dust a work surface with flour and roll out the puff pastry about ⅛ inch [4 mm] thick. Place an upside-down plate on the pastry and use the tip of a sharp knife to cut out a 10-inch [25 cm] circle. Transfer the circle to the top of the leek mixture and tuck the edges of the pastry around the carrots. Cut three small slits into the pastry. Sprinkle with pepper and bake until the puff pastry is very browned and firm, 45 minutes to 1 hour.

Let the tarte cool for 5 minutes, then carefully turn out onto a round serving plate. Serve warm or at room temperature.

FRITES

Serves 4 to 6

3 pounds [1.4 kg] large
Yukon gold potatoes,
peeled

6 to 7 cups [1.4 to 1.7 L]
vegetable oil

Fine sea salt

My very first date with a woman was over frites and red wine at a sidewalk café in Paris. (Absolutely ridiculous, I know.) "Frites" is French for fries and—unless you're in Belgium, where they are thick-cut and very potato-y—they come in all shapes, from very thin to very Belgian. My preference for home-cooked frites lies in the middle ground and attempts to avoid oil burns at all costs. To do so, I start with the cut potatoes already in cold oil and let it all heat up and come to a boil together. This results in crisp, golden frites that I still love best when paired with a pour of red wine and some awkward flirting.

Square off the potatoes by cutting a ¼-inch [6 mm] slice from each of their four long sides; discard the slices. Cut the potatoes lengthwise into ¼-inch [6 mm] slabs. Stack three or four slabs and cut lengthwise into ¼-inch [6 mm] fries. Repeat with the remaining potatoes.

Line a baking sheet with paper towels. In a large Dutch oven or pot over high heat, combine the potatoes and oil. Bring the oil to a boil. Adjust the heat to maintain a steady boil and cook, without stirring, until the outsides of the potatoes begin to firm, 15 to 20 minutes. Use a pair of tongs to gently stir the potatoes and continue cooking until the potatoes are golden and crisp, 15 to 20 minutes more.

Transfer the fries to the prepared baking sheet with a slotted spoon and season with salt. Serve hot.

POTATOES, ARTICHOKES + SHALLOTS

Serves 4 to 6

3 pounds [1.4 kg] waxy potatoes, cut into 1½-inch [4 cm] dice

One 8-ounce [230 g] jar artichoke hearts packed in oil, drained and halved lengthwise

6 small shallots, halved lengthwise

3 tablespoons salted capers, soaked, rinsed, and drained

¼ cup [60 ml] extra-virgin olive oil

Fine sea salt

Freshly ground black pepper

2 tablespoons apple cider vinegar

You could certainly do the work to turn a bunch of artichokes for this recipe (see page 150), or you could just buy a jar of already prepared hearts packed in oil and luxuriate in all the extra time you have to make something else labor-intensive for your dinner party. Added bonus of the aforementioned shortcut: You get to use some of the flavor-packed artichoke oil to roast everything in.

Preheat the oven to 425°F [220°C].

On a large baking sheet, combine the potatoes, artichoke hearts, shallots, and capers. Drizzle with the olive oil and 2 tablespoons of the oil the artichokes were packed in; season with salt and pepper. Toss to coat. Roast until the potatoes are browned and tender, 45 minutes to 1 hour, tossing halfway through. Drizzle with the vinegar and serve warm.

POMMES ANNA

Serves 6

9 tablespoons [130 g] unsalted European butter, melted, plus more for buttering the foil

3½ pounds [1.6 kg] russet potatoes, peeled and cut into ⅛-inch [4 mm] slices, patted dry with paper towels

1½ teaspoons fine sea salt, plus more as needed

Note

In pursuit of keeping this recipe as close to the original as possible, I didn't include a thing I often do right before serving it at home: an actual pile of finely grated Mimolette cheese. The salty-sweet, nutty hit of bright-orange, creamy cow's milk cheese is really, really, really special on top of sizzling, buttery, crisp-edged potatoes.

Every single time I make pommes Anna for French friends, they have absolutely no idea what I've made. Don't get me wrong, they love it, but it's the buttery, crispy-edged layers of potatoes they love—not the nostalgia. It's a true shame that this nineteenth-century recipe doesn't see much play on French tables anymore, because pommes Anna is a three-ingredient recipe and one of those ingredients is butter.

The original was created at Café Anglais in Paris and said to be named after Anna Deslions, a courtesan who entertained dignitaries in a private salon above the elaborately decorated dining room. While I don't know much about the OG Anna, the dish created in her honor requires dousing layers of paper-thin potato slices with butter and pressing it all together to create something like a cake that is crisp outside and soft inside. Anna did something right.

Preheat the oven to 425°F [220°C].

Add 3 tablespoons of the melted butter to a 10-inch [25 cm] cast-iron skillet. Add one-third of the potato slices in a circular pattern, overlapping them slightly. Brush with 2 tablespoons of the butter and sprinkle with ½ teaspoon of the salt.

Make two more layers with the remaining potatoes, butter, and salt, piling any remaining potatoes in the center (this will create an even pommes Anna after everything is cooked). Set over medium heat and cook, without moving the pan, for 10 minutes.

Butter one side of a piece of aluminum foil and cover the pan, buttered-side down. Use a 9-inch [23 cm] cake pan to press down firmly on the potatoes. Remove the cake pan and place the skillet in the oven for 20 minutes. Remove the skillet and again use the cake pan to press the potatoes down firmly. Remove the foil and continue to bake until the potatoes are tender and the top is deeply browned, about 30 minutes more.

Let rest for 10 minutes, then run a thin spatula around the edges and bottom of the skillet and flip it carefully onto a serving platter so the golden bottom faces up. Serve warm.

GRATIN DAUPHINOIS (A.K.A. FRENCH SCALLOPED POTATOES)

Serves 6

2 pounds [910 g] waxy potatoes, peeled and cut into ⅛-inch [4 mm] slices on a mandoline

1½ cups [360 ml] whole milk

½ cup [120 ml] heavy cream

1 garlic clove, smashed

1 bay leaf

1½ teaspoons fine sea salt

Pinch of freshly grated nutmeg

½ tablespoon unsalted European butter

3 tablespoons grated Gruyère cheese (optional)

Gratin Dauphinois is a pretty way to describe very simple, very rich scalloped potatoes. Note the original, from the Dauphiné region of southeastern France, doesn't involve any cheese. If you want to stick with traditional, leave the cheese off. (I'm not really sure why anyone would ever "leave the cheese off," but to each her own.)

In a large saucepan over medium heat, combine the potatoes, milk, cream, garlic, bay leaf, salt, and nutmeg. Bring to a simmer, lower the heat, and continue to simmer, stirring frequently, until the potatoes start to soften but are not cooked through, 8 to 10 minutes. Remove and discard the garlic and bay leaf.

Preheat the oven to 375°F [190°C]. Butter a 12-inch [30.5 cm] shallow gratin dish or two smaller dishes if you're splitting the potato mixture.

Add the potatoes in an even layer. Sprinkle with the Gruyère (if using). Bake until bubbling and browned on top, 50 minutes to 1 hour. Serve warm.

ALIGOT (MASHED POTATOES WITH CHEESE)

Serves 6

3 pounds [1.4 kg] Yukon gold potatoes, peeled and quartered

1 cup [240 g] crème fraîche or sour cream

6 tablespoons [90 g] unsalted European butter, cut into cubes

1 pound [455 g] fresh mozzarella, cut into cubes

8 ounces [230 g] Comté or Gruyère cheese, grated

Fine sea salt

Two things. One: The French say you can't make aligot ("ah-lee-go") without either tomme de Laguiole or tomme d'Auvergne, two semisoft fresh cheeses from the Aveyron region of France, which, like many hyper-local, hyper-special, hyper-French things, you can't find in the United States. Two: I say you can't make a good aligot without a ricer or a food mill and I have tried, trust me. *But* rich, fondue-slash-mashed-potatoes-but-make-it-classy aligot is worth finding a way around at least one of these issues. If you can't or won't visit France and take some liberty with customs regulations on your return, a combination of Comté for flavor and fresh mozzarella for elastic pull gets close enough to justify digging out, borrowing, or buying a ricer or food mill.

Add the potatoes to a large pot and cover them with cold water. Bring to a boil over high heat and cook until they are very tender, 15 to 20 minutes. Drain the potatoes, taking care to tip out any excess water in the pot, and pass the hot potatoes through a ricer or food mill back into the pot. Turn the heat to very low and stir the potatoes to allow any excess water to evaporate. Stir in the crème fraîche and butter until the butter melts.

Add half the mozzarella and half the Comté to the pot and stir vigorously with a large wooden spoon, making a figure-eight pattern. Once the cheese is incorporated, add the remaining cheese and continue to beat the mixture vigorously until the cheese is completely melted, the aligot begins to pull away from the sides of the pan, and when you lift the spoon, it makes long, stretchy, cheesy strands. Season with salt, transfer to a warmed serving dish, and serve immediately.

BEANS WITH PISTACHIO AÏLLADE

Serves 6 to 8

Beans

1¼ cups [200 g] dried cannellini beans, picked over, soaked overnight, and drained

6 garlic cloves, smashed

3 tablespoons extra-virgin olive oil

1 bay leaf

Fine sea salt

Aïllade

1 cup plus 2 tablespoons [160 g] shelled unsalted pistachios

2 garlic cloves

½ teaspoon fine sea salt, plus more as needed

2 tablespoons rosé wine

½ lemon, zested

11 tablespoons [160 ml] extra-virgin olive oil

Aïllade is a simple sauce from the Languedoc region of southern France made by pounding together garlic, nuts, wine, and zest. You can use walnuts or hazelnuts, but I much prefer the subtle, sweet flavor and muted color of pistachios in my aïllade. You can also put it on something altogether different, such as pasta or pork chops or grilled summer vegetables, but the truth is we should all be finding reasons to eat more beans.

To make the beans: In a large saucepan over medium-high heat, combine the drained beans, garlic, oil, bay leaf, and 6 cups [1.4 L] of water. Bring to a boil, then lower the heat, season with salt, and simmer until the beans are tender but the skins are still intact, about 1 hour.

While the beans cook, make the aïllade: In a large skillet over medium heat, add the pistachios and cook, tossing, until they are just warmed through, about 3 minutes. Remove and reserve 2 tablespoons of the pistachios.

If you are making the aïllade with a mortar and pestle: Place the garlic and salt in a mortar and pestle and grind until a paste forms. Add 1 cup [140 g] of the pistachios and pound them, scraping the sides of the mortar often, until they are smashed into small pieces. Add the rosé and lemon zest and stir to mix. Slowly add the oil, 1 tablespoon at a time, smashing until it's all combined. Season with salt.

If you are making the aïllade with a food processor: Place the garlic cloves in the bowl of a food processor and pulse until roughly chopped. Add 1 cup [140 g] of the pistachios and the salt and pulse, scraping the sides of the food processor often, until they are ground into small pieces. Add the rosé and lemon zest and pulse just to mix. With the food processor running, slowly pour in the oil until it's all combined. Season with salt.

Transfer the beans to a serving bowl. Add the aïllade and toss to coat. If the mixture looks dry, add a bit of the bean cooking liquid. Sprinkle with the reserved 2 tablespoons of pistachios; serve warm or at room temperature.

BEANS LONGTEMPS

Serves 6 to 8

1½ cups [240 g] white beans such as Tarbais or cannellini, picked over, soaked overnight, and drained

1 large yellow onion, halved

7 garlic cloves

2 bay leaves

¼ cup [55 g] tomato paste

3 tablespoons extra-virgin olive oil

1½ pounds [680 g] heirloom tomatoes, coarsely chopped

Fine sea salt

Freshly ground black pepper

2 tablespoons red wine vinegar

½ cup [120 ml] dry red wine

Pinch of red pepper flakes

4 tablespoons [55 g] unsalted European butter

1 cup [140 g] bread crumbs

¼ cup [10 g] finely chopped fresh flat-leaf parsley

I've been told multiple times, in no uncertain terms, that you don't put bread crumbs on cassoulet—one that is well made should develop a crust on its own in the oven. And so, my Cassoulet (page 142) is bread crumb–less. But here's the thing: I love beans topped with a crunchy, buttery layer of garlicky bread crumbs. Since it's technically not cassoulet, my French guests won't take offense, plus it's vegetarian—vegan if you cut the butter, which you can totally do (but unless you're actually vegan or having vegan guests over, please don't). Everything is cooked for a long time (longtemps), so make this the morning of or—if you want the flavors to be even more wonderful—the day before you're planning to serve it and reheat.

In a large pot over medium heat, combine the beans, one of the onion halves, four of the garlic cloves, the bay leaves, tomato paste, and 8 cups [2 L] of water. Bring to a boil, then lower the heat to a simmer and cook until the beans are tender and cooked through, 1½ to 2 hours for the Tarbais, 45 minutes to 1 hour for the cannellini. Set aside to cool in their cooking liquid.

Thinly slice the remaining onion half and two of the garlic cloves. In another large ovenproof pot or Dutch oven over medium heat, add the oil. Once the oil is hot, add the onions and the sliced garlic and cook, stirring often, until tender, 5 to 7 minutes. Add the tomatoes, season with salt and pepper, and cook for 3 minutes, then stir in the vinegar and cook for 1 minute more. Stir in the beans and their cooking liquid, the red wine, and red pepper flakes. Season with salt and pepper and bring to a boil. Lower the heat and simmer until the sauce is thickened, about 30 minutes. Stir in 1 tablespoon of the butter and taste for seasoning. Remove from the heat.

Preheat the oven to 325°F [165°C].

Finely chop the remaining garlic clove. In a small skillet over medium heat, melt the remaining 3 tablespoons of butter. Add the garlic and cook, stirring, until toasted, about 1 minute. Stir in the bread crumbs and season with salt and pepper. Remove the pan from the heat and stir in the parsley. Sprinkle the bread crumb mixture over the beans and bake until the bread crumbs are golden and the dish is heated through, 20 to 30 minutes. Serve warm.

AFTER

(SWEET) SNACKS + POST-DINNER DRINKS

AFTER ————————————————————

Desserts

————————

*REMARQUE

Digestifs

*REMARQUE

DESSERTS

STRAWBERRIES + CRÈME

Serves 4

1 pound [455 g] fresh strawberries, stemmed and large berries halved

1 tablespoon sugar

Pinch of fine sea salt

½ cup [120 ml] heavy cream

¼ cup [60 g] crème fraîche

Shortbread or sablés (store-bought or page 263), crumbled

Flaky sea salt

I grew up on strawberries as dessert, picked fresh and sun-warm from my grandmother's garden, topped in the early years with Cool Whip, later with freshly whipped cream. This crème fraîche–laced variation is my French version, eaten the moment strawberries hit the Paris markets (late April or May, if you want to plan a trip around it) through the very end of the season. If you're using truly ripe strawberries, you shouldn't need much sugar—it's meant more to pull out their juices than to actually sweeten. If you're making this in a shoulder season with less-than-perfect berries, adjust the amount of sugar to taste.

Place a large metal bowl and whisk in the freezer to chill for 10 minutes.

In a medium bowl, combine the strawberries, sugar, and fine sea salt. Set aside to macerate while you make the crème.

In the chilled bowl, add the heavy cream and crème fraîche. Whisk until medium peaks form, 4 to 6 minutes.

To serve, transfer the fruit to small serving bowls or plates. Dollop with the crème, drizzle with the accumulated strawberry juice, and top with shortbread crumbles. Sprinkle with flaky salt and serve immediately.

APRICOT CRUMBLE

**Makes one
10-inch [25 cm]
crumble**

Filling

1½ pounds [680 g] ripe apricots, halved and pitted

½ cup [100 g] granulated sugar

2 tablespoons dry rosé wine

1 tablespoon all-purpose flour

½ lemon, zested and juiced

½ vanilla bean, split and scraped, pod reserved for another use

Pinch of fine sea salt

Crumble

1½ cups [210 g] all-purpose flour

1 cup [200 g] packed dark brown sugar

¾ cup [165 g] unsalted European butter, melted, plus more for greasing the pan

½ teaspoon finely chopped fresh rosemary

½ teaspoon fine sea salt

Flaky sea salt

The keys to taking this from *a crumble* to *a crumble no one wants to stop eating* is picking extremely ripe fruit and baking it longer than you think you should. This gives the filling time to bubble through so much that it starts to caramelize and merge with the savory brown sugar crumble topping, resulting in deep flavors and an addictive, candy-like texture.

Preheat the oven to 400°F [200°C].

To make the filling: In a medium bowl, combine the apricots, granulated sugar, rosé, flour, lemon zest and juice, vanilla bean seeds, and fine sea salt. Stir to combine and set aside.

To make the crumble: In another medium bowl, stir together the flour, brown sugar, melted butter, rosemary, and fine sea salt. The mixture should be wet and clumpy.

Butter a 10-inch [25 cm] round cake pan or baking dish and add the filling mixture to the prepared pan. Use your hands to clump the topping together into pieces and scatter it across the top of the apricots. Sprinkle with flaky salt. Bake until the filling is bubbling and the top crust is golden and set, 45 to 55 minutes. If the top is browning too quickly, cover with aluminum foil for the last 15 to 20 minutes. Serve warm or at room temperature.

FIG CLAFOUTIS

Serves 6

1 tablespoon unsalted European butter, melted

1½ pounds [680 g] fresh figs, stemmed and halved

1 cup [240 ml] whole milk

¼ cup [60 ml] heavy cream

3 large eggs

⅓ cup plus 1 tablespoon [80 g] sugar

1 teaspoon vanilla extract

½ teaspoon fine sea salt

½ cup [70 g] all-purpose flour

Flaky sea salt

It's slightly arrogant to dictate what you do with figs during fig season, so I'll tell you what *I* do: I eat them. I eat them immediately after buying, usually as I walk back home. If I've gotten enough, I eat more when I get home. If I've *really* gotten enough, I make this.

Preheat the oven to 350°F [180°C].

Brush the bottom of a 12-inch [30.5 cm] baking dish with butter and add the figs in a single layer.

In a large bowl, whisk together the milk, heavy cream, eggs, ⅓ cup [65 g] of the sugar, the vanilla, and fine sea salt until the sugar is dissolved. Add the flour and whisk until smooth. Pour the mixture over the figs and sprinkle with the remaining 1 tablespoon of sugar. Bake until the top is puffed and browned and the custard is set, 60 to 75 minutes. Sprinkle with flaky salt and serve warm or at room temperature.

(MY FIRST) FRENCH (GIRLFRIEND'S) APPLE TART

Serves 6 to 8

All-purpose flour, for dusting

One 14-ounce [400 g] package all-butter puff pastry

4 medium apples, peeled, cored, and thinly sliced

2 tablespoons sugar

1 teaspoon ground cinnamon

2 tablespoons salted European butter, cut into small pieces

2 tablespoons apricot preserves, warmed

Flaky sea salt

Whipped cream, for serving (optional)

The first dinner party I threw in Paris doubled as my fourth date with my first French girlfriend. She made this very classic, very French apple tart, and while the relationship ended a few months later, this recipe and I have been going strong for years.

Preheat the oven to 400°F [200°C]. Line a baking sheet with parchment paper.

Lightly dust a clean work surface with flour and roll out the puff pastry into a circle about ¼ inch [6 mm] thick. Transfer the circle to the prepared baking sheet and use a fork to prick the pastry all over. Lay the apple slices in an even layer across the puff pastry however you prefer, making sure to overlap the slices slightly. Sprinkle with the sugar and cinnamon. Dot with the butter pieces. Bake until the edges of the apples and the puff pastry are golden brown, 35 to 40 minutes. Remove the tart and immediately brush with the warm preserves and sprinkle with flaky salt. Serve warm or at room temperature with whipped cream, if desired.

CHERRY GALETTE

**Makes one
12-inch [30.5 cm]
galette**

Crust

1½ cups [210 g]
unbleached all-purpose
flour, plus more for dusting

1 tablespoon sugar

½ teaspoon fine sea salt

½ lemon, zested

½ cup [110 g] unsalted
European butter, chilled
and cubed

Filling

1¼ pounds [570 g] fresh
cherries, stemmed and
pitted

2 tablespoons plus
1 teaspoon sugar

1 tablespoon cornstarch

½ lemon, zested

½ teaspoon vanilla extract,
or 1 vanilla bean, split and
scraped, pod reserved for
another use

½ teaspoon fine sea salt

1 egg, lightly beaten

¼ teaspoon flaky sea salt

Heavy cream, chilled, for
serving

You know what people around a table really lose their minds over? The pouring of good cold cream over a dessert. Try it first on this galette, which is studded with cherries enclosed in a flaky, lightly citrus crust, then keep a pint in the refrigerator for your next chocolate cake, batch of brownies, literally any ripe fresh or roasted fruit, a pie or tart . . . you get the idea.

To make the crust: In a food processor or large bowl, combine the flour, sugar, and fine sea salt. Add the lemon zest and cubed butter and pulse, or use your hands to press together until pea-size pieces form. Add 3 to 5 tablespoons [45 to 80 ml] of ice water and mix just until a dough forms. Gather into a ball and wrap in plastic or reusable beeswax wrap. Refrigerate for at least 1 hour and up to 3 days.

To make the filling: In a large bowl, combine the cherries, 2 tablespoons of the sugar, cornstarch, lemon zest, vanilla, and fine sea salt. Toss to combine.

Preheat the oven to 400°F [200°C].

On a lightly floured piece of parchment paper, roll out the dough into a 15-inch [38 cm] circle. Slide the parchment onto a large rimmed baking sheet and use a pastry brush to brush the dough with the beaten egg (reserving some egg to finish). Mound the prepared cherry filling in the center of the dough, leaving a 2- to 3-inch [5 to 7.5 cm] border. Gently fold the edges of the dough up and over most of the fruit, pressing the folds gently to seal.

Brush the folded edges of the galette with the remaining beaten egg. Sprinkle with the remaining 1 teaspoon of sugar and flaky sea salt. Bake for 20 minutes. Lower the oven temperature to 350°F [180°C] and continue baking until the crust is golden brown and the filling is bubbly and nearly set, 40 to 50 minutes. Let the galette cool on the baking sheet on a cooling rack (the liquid will continue to set as it cools). Serve warm or at room temperature, drizzled with cold cream.

KOUIGN-AMANN

Makes one 9-inch [23-cm] cake

2 tablespoons active dry yeast

1 cup plus 1 tablespoon [250 g] all-purpose flour, plus more for dusting

1½ teaspoons flaky sea salt, plus more for sprinkling

15 tablespoons [200 g] salted European butter, cubed

1 cup [200 g] sugar

Note

If you want to serve this cake warm—but also want to enjoy your dinner party—bake it earlier in the day, place on a parchment-lined baking sheet, and reheat in a 325°F [165°C] oven for 5 to 10 minutes.

À TABLE

The first time I had a kouign-amann, I was in wild, beautiful, coastal Finistère (in the westernmost part of Brittany) for a friend's wedding. I left honored to bear witness to love and saddened I didn't take another slice of the buttery Breton pastry for the drive back to Paris. Because here's the thing about most regional specialties in France: You often cannot find them outside their region and even if you do, they're often not nearly as good. Don't let its pronunciation (it's "queen-AH-mahn") or the idea of working with a laminated dough discourage you. Kouign-amann is exactly what it says it is: kouign = cake; amann = butter. Emphasis on butter. Get the best you can find, plan a day ahead (the dough needs to rest overnight in the refrigerator), and watch as five (six, counting water) simple ingredients transform into sweet, buttery, salty, soft, flaky, crunchy, caramelized layers of perfection.

In the bowl of a stand mixer fitted with a hook attachment, combine the yeast and ⅔ cup [150 ml] of lukewarm water. Set aside for 3 minutes to dissolve the yeast. Add the flour and salt to the stand mixer and stir to combine, adding more lukewarm water if needed (the dough should be moist but not wet). Knead on low speed until a smooth ball forms (it should be tacky to the touch but not overly sticky), about 10 minutes, then shape the dough into a round and cover with a damp kitchen towel; refrigerate overnight.

The next day, take the butter out of the refrigerator and let sit at room temperature for 1 hour.

Preheat the oven to 350°F [180°C].

Sandwich the butter between two sheets of parchment paper and use a rolling pin to shape it into a 5-inch [12 cm] square, about ½ inch [12 cm] thick. Set aside.

Lightly dust a work surface with flour and gently transfer the chilled dough to the surface. Gently roll the dough into a 10-inch [25 cm] square and add the butter square to the center of the dough square. Working quickly, fold the dough over the edges to completely encase the butter, pinching at the seams.

Flip the dough-butter package over, re-flour the surface if necessary, and gently roll the package into an 18-by-10-inch [46 by 25 cm] rectangle, about ½ inch [12 mm] thick.

Sprinkle the top evenly with about half of the sugar and use the rolling pin to lightly press the sugar into the dough. Turn the dough so that the shorter side is nearest you and fold into thirds, as you would a letter. Turn the package 90 degrees and immediately roll into another 18-by-10-inch [46 by 25 cm] rectangle, about ½ inch [12 mm] thick. Sprinkle with the rest of the sugar, reserving 2 tablespoons.

Use the rolling pin to lightly press the sugar into the dough. Turn the dough so that the shorter side is nearest you and again fold into thirds. Gently roll the dough into a 10-inch [25 cm] square and use your hands to push in each of the corners to bundle into a rough circle, the same size as a 9-inch [23 cm] cake pan. Use a sharp paring knife to score the dough in a crisscross pattern, cutting about ¼ inch [6 mm] into the dough.

Line a 9-inch [23 cm] cake pan with parchment paper, letting it come up the sides of the pan. Sprinkle with the reserved 2 tablespoons of sugar. Flip the cake into the pan, scored-side down, and bake until the top is very deeply browned, 55 to 65 minutes.

Set a cooling rack on a rimmed baking sheet. Set a large plate over the cake pan and carefully flip the hot cake onto the plate. Discard the parchment paper. Carefully transfer the cake, scored-side up, to the cooling rack. Sprinkle with flaky salt and set aside to cool for 30 minutes. Serve warm or at room temperature.

ALSATIAN CHEESECAKE

Makes one 9-inch [23 cm] cheesecake

Crust

1½ cups [210 g] unbleached all-purpose flour, plus more for dusting

1 tablespoon granulated sugar

½ teaspoon fine sea salt

½ cup [110 g] unsalted European butter, chilled and cubed

Filling

1½ cups [360 g] fromage blanc

¼ cup [60 ml] heavy cream

3 large eggs, separated and at room temperature

½ cup plus 3 tablespoons [145 g] granulated sugar

¼ cup [35 g] cornstarch, sifted

½ teaspoon fine sea salt

1 tablespoon vanilla extract

Confectioners' sugar, for dusting

I went to a French pastry school in New York City before I moved to Paris, so what I'm saying is, woman knows her cheesecake. This Alsatian version is *just* reminiscent enough of New York's Junior's but less sweet and less dense, and it skips the graham crackers for a crust made of pie dough. Still, though, it goes very well with jammy, sugared cherries, should you be into that sort of thing.

To make the crust: In a food processor or large bowl, combine the flour, granulated sugar, and salt. Add the cubed butter and pulse, or use your hands to press together until pea-size pieces form. Add 3 to 5 tablespoons [45 to 80 ml] of ice water and mix just until a dough forms. Gather into a ball and wrap in plastic or reusable beeswax wrap. Refrigerate for at least 1 hour and up to 3 days.

Lightly butter a 9-inch [23 cm] springform pan.

On a lightly floured surface, roll out the dough into a 15-inch [38 cm] circle. Transfer to the springform pan and gently press the dough into the base and sides of the pan. Trim the edges and prick the bottom of the dough all over with a fork. Refrigerate the dough for 30 minutes.

Preheat the oven to 400°F [200°C].

Line the dough with parchment paper and add dried beans or pie weights. Bake for 20 minutes, then remove the paper and weights and continue to bake until the crust is nicely golden brown, 10 to 15 minutes more. Set aside to cool.

cont'd

Lower the oven temperature to 350°F [180°C].

To make the filling: While the crust cools, in a large bowl, whisk together the fromage blanc and heavy cream. Whisk in the egg yolks one at a time, whisking until combined. Whisk in ½ cup [100 g] of the granulated sugar, the cornstarch, salt, and vanilla.

In the bowl of a stand mixer fitted with the whisk attachment, beat the egg whites until foamy. Beating constantly on medium speed, slowly add the remaining 3 tablespoons of granulated sugar. Increase the speed to medium-high and continue to beat just until glossy soft peaks form, about 2 minutes more.

Add a generous spoonful of the whipped egg whites to the fromage blanc mixture and use a spatula to stir to combine. Gently fold in the rest of the egg whites, just until combined.

Add the filling to the crust and bake until the top is golden and set, 55 to 70 minutes. (If the top is browning too quickly, cover gently with aluminum foil.) Set aside to cool completely in the pan, then chill for at least 2 hours and up to overnight. Carefully remove from the pan, and dust with confectioners' sugar just before serving.

EXPAT YOGURT CAKE

**Makes one
9-by-5-inch
[23 by 12 cm] loaf**

Crumble Topping

½ cup [70 g] all-purpose
flour

¼ cup [50 g] packed dark
brown sugar

2 teaspoons poppy seeds

1 teaspoon fine sea salt

4 tablespoons [55 g] chilled
unsalted European butter,
cut into ¼-inch [6 mm]
cubes

Cake

1½ cups [210 g] all-purpose
flour

¼ cup [35 g] poppy seeds

2 teaspoons baking powder

1 teaspoon fine sea salt

1 cup [200 g] granulated
sugar

⅔ cup [160 g] whole milk
Greek yogurt

3 large eggs

1 tablespoon vanilla extract

½ cup [120 ml] mild extra-
virgin olive oil

Flaky sea salt

Note
You can also bake these in a
standard, 12-cup muffin tin,
buttered or lined with paper
muffin cups. Shorten the
baking time (a lot) to 15 to
18 minutes (or until a toothpick
inserted in the center comes
out clean).

In a land of bakeries on every block, there's not always ample
reason to bake at home in France. But even in the least
ambitious baker's home is a stained recipe card for French
yogurt cake. Made with not much more than eggs, sugar, flour,
oil, and—mais oui—yogurt, it's as easy as box mix and ideal
for Sunday brunches, teatime, birthdays, and Tuesdays. The
classic recipe does not include poppy seeds or a crumble
topping, but it should, so I'm playing the expat card here.
Serve à la française with a little crème fraîche on the side.

Preheat the oven to 350°F [180°C]. Line a loaf pan with one long
piece of parchment paper overhanging either long side of the
pan. Set aside.

To make the crumble topping: In a medium bowl, combine the
flour, brown sugar, poppy seeds, and fine sea salt. Scatter the
butter cubes on top and use your hands to combine until large
clumps form.

To make the cake: In a medium bowl, whisk together the flour,
poppy seeds, baking powder, and fine sea salt. Set aside.

In another medium bowl, whisk together the granulated sugar,
yogurt, eggs, and vanilla. Add the oil and whisk just to combine.
Add the dry ingredients and use a rubber spatula to fold
together. Scrape the batter into the prepared pan. Scatter the
crumble topping over and sprinkle with flaky sea salt.

Transfer the pan to the oven and bake until golden brown and
a toothpick inserted in the center comes out clean, 55 to
65 minutes (cover the top loosely with aluminum foil if the
cake is browning too quickly).

Remove the pan from the oven and set aside to rest for
10 minutes. Use the parchment sides to lift the cake from the
pan and let cool completely on a cooling rack before slicing
and serving.

MACADAMIA NUT BRITTLE ICE CREAM

**Makes 1 quart
[1 L]
(plus extra brittle)**

Ice Cream

2 cups [480 ml] whole milk

1 cup [240 ml] heavy whipping cream

½ teaspoon fine sea salt

6 large egg yolks

⅔ cup [150 g] sugar

2 teaspoons vanilla extract

Macadamia Nut Brittle

1 cup [200 g] sugar

1 cup [260 g] macadamia nuts, toasted and coarsely chopped

2 teaspoons vanilla extract

2 teaspoons flaky sea salt

Note

Use some of the extra egg whites from this recipe to make Macaroons (page 269).

Discontinued in the United States, Häagen-Dazs's Macadamia Nut Brittle is the only prepackaged ice cream I buy in France. This is my version, which makes extra brittle because life is short, folks.

To make the ice cream: Prepare an ice bath in a large bowl and set aside. In a large saucepan over low heat, add the milk, cream, and fine sea salt and heat gently, stirring occasionally, until the mixture is hot but not boiling.

In a medium bowl, whisk together the egg yolks and sugar until pale. Whisking constantly, slowly add half of the milk mixture to the eggs. Return this to the pan with the rest of the milk mixture. Add the vanilla and cook over low heat, stirring often, until the custard thickens enough to coat the back of a wooden spoon. Pour the custard into a bowl and set in the prepared ice bath. Cool completely, stirring occasionally, then cover with plastic or reusable beeswax wrap and chill for at least 6 hours and up to overnight.

To make the brittle: Butter a baking sheet or line with a silicone baking mat.

In a large saucepan over medium heat, combine the sugar and 2 tablespoons of water. Stir to combine, then bring to a low boil and cook, swirling the pan occasionally, until the mixture is golden brown, 5 to 7 minutes.

Stir in the macadamia nuts, vanilla, and flaky salt. Immediately pour the mixture onto the prepared baking sheet and spread it out with a silicone spatula. Cool at room temperature, then chop into irregular small pieces.

Pour the chilled custard into an ice cream machine and churn according to the manufacturer's instructions. Add about half of the brittle pieces (reserve the rest for snacking or another batch of ice cream) just at the end to combine, then serve immediately for a soft-serve consistency or spoon into a pint container and store in the freezer until ready to serve.

CHOCOLATE PUDDING, BUT FRENCH

Serves 6 to 8

2½ cups [600 ml] whole milk

¾ cup [180 ml] heavy cream

½ cup [100 g] sugar

3 tablespoons cornstarch, sifted

1 vanilla bean, split and scraped, pod reserved for another use

1 teaspoon vanilla extract

Heaping ¼ teaspoon fine sea salt

3 large eggs, at room temperature

3½ ounces [100 g] dark chocolate, coarsely chopped

3½ ounces [100 g] white chocolate, coarsely chopped

Lightly whipped cream, for serving

Flaky sea salt, for serving

Note
This can be portioned into individual pots for serving, but ask yourself this: Do you like fun?

Chocolate is messy and finicky and—please keep reading this book/recipe after you hear this—unless it's in strict bar form, I don't particularly like it for dessert. A great many in France, however, do. This recipe takes their pudding-like pots de crème and their rich, family-style bowls of mousse au chocolat and combines them with a chocolate-based American schoolyard treat I do love: layered pudding cups. Serve it in your biggest, chicest bowl with lots of whipped cream, flaky salt, and spoons.

In a medium saucepan over medium-high heat, add the milk, cream, sugar, cornstarch, vanilla bean seeds, vanilla extract, and fine sea salt and bring to a boil, whisking constantly. Let the mixture boil just until it starts to thicken, 1½ to 2 minutes, then immediately remove the pan from the heat.

In a medium bowl, whisk the eggs. Whisking constantly, slowly add ½ cup [120 ml] of the hot milk mixture to the eggs. Pour it all back into the pan with the remaining milk mixture and cook, whisking constantly over low heat, until the mixture just starts to bubble.

Place the dark chocolate in one mixing bowl and the white chocolate in another. Strain half the milk mixture through a fine-mesh sieve into each bowl. Whisk both until the chocolates are completely melted and the puddings are smooth.

Transfer the dark chocolate pudding to a large serving bowl. Add the white chocolate pudding and gently swirl just to barely combine. Refrigerate until chilled and firm, at least 6 hours, and serve with lightly whipped cream and flaky salt.

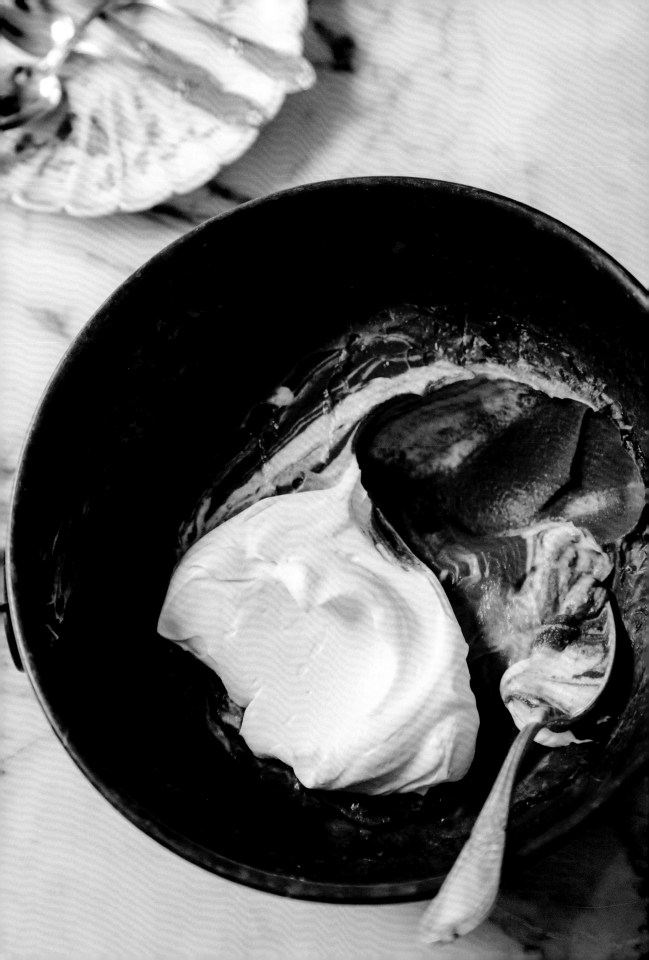

SABLÉS, BUT NOT, LIKE, REGULAR SABLÉS, COOL SABLÉS

Makes 64 cookies

1 cup [220 g] unsalted European butter

½ cup [60 g] confectioners' sugar

¼ cup [50 g] granulated sugar

1 vanilla bean, split and scraped, pod reserved for another use

3 large egg yolks, at room temperature

1 teaspoon vanilla extract

2¼ cups [315 g] all-purpose flour

1 teaspoon flaky sea salt, plus more for sprinkling

1 egg white, lightly beaten

⅓ cup [65 g] turbinado sugar

One of the fun things about being an American living in Europe is that many parts of fairly innocuous American culture suddenly become hip. Take drop cookies. Your chocolate chip, your peanut butter, your white chocolate macadamia: All have become très cool in Paris. But the French forget their own best cookie. Sablés are simple, crumbly ("sablé" means sandy), two-bite cookies rich with butter and not much else, just as good freshly baked as they are a few days later. This recipe is an update on the classic with extra vanilla and salt and a coating of turbinado sugar.

In a stand mixer fitted with a paddle attachment, combine the butter, confectioners' and granulated sugars, and vanilla bean seeds; beat until light and fluffy. Add the egg yolks and vanilla extract and beat until the eggs are incorporated. Stir in the flour and salt just until combined.

Divide the dough in half and form each half into a 10-by-1½-inch [25 by 4 cm] log. Wrap in parchment paper and refrigerate for at least 2 hours and up to 3 days. (The logs can also be frozen for up to 3 months.)

Preheat the oven to 350°F [180°C].

Working one at a time, unwrap the logs and brush the outsides with the egg white, reserving some for brushing each sablé. Sprinkle with the turbinado sugar until completely coated. Use a sharp knife to cut each log into 32 thin slices (about ¼-inch [6 mm] thick) and transfer to a baking sheet, cut-sides down. Brush the tops of the cookies with the egg white and sprinkle with additional turbinado sugar and flaky salt. Bake until the sablés are set and lightly golden around the edges, 12 to 15 minutes. Cookies will last, stored in an airtight container, for up to 5 days.

THIBAULT'S MADELEINES

Makes 24 madeleines

1 cup [140 g] all-purpose flour, plus more for dusting the pans

1 teaspoon baking powder

½ teaspoon fine sea salt

⅔ cup [130 g] sugar

½ vanilla bean, split and scraped, pod reserved for another use

3 large eggs, at room temperature

½ cup [110 g] unsalted European butter, melted and cooled slightly, plus more for greasing the pans

1 tablespoon vanilla extract

While there's ample room for a lovely lady lumps pun here, I'll spare you. All you need to know is that these small, tender, classic French cookie-cakes are packed with so much vanilla that they taste like birthday cake and—as long as you follow the steps—you'll get those coveted L.L.L. every time.

In a small bowl, whisk together the flour, baking powder, and salt.

In a medium bowl, combine the sugar and vanilla bean seeds, then add the eggs and vigorously whisk until the mixture is smooth and lightly thickened. Use a spatula to fold in the dry ingredients just until they are incorporated. Add the melted butter and vanilla extract and fold gently to combine.

Butter and lightly flour two madeleine pans (or work in batches and chill the remaining half of the batter), and spoon the batter into the molds until each mold is about two-thirds full (you may have a little batter left over). Cover the pan lightly with a sheet of parchment paper and refrigerate for at least 2 hours and up to overnight.

Place a large, heavy baking sheet on the middle rack of the oven and preheat the oven to 450°F [230°C].

Place the cold madeleine pan on the hot baking sheet and lower the oven temperature to 350°F [180°C]. Bake until the edges of the madeleines are golden brown and the centers lightly spring back when gently poked, about 10 minutes. Assertively tap the bottom edge of the pan against the counter to release the madeleines from their molds and carefully transfer to a serving platter. Serve immediately.

TEURGOULE (BAKED RICE PUDDING FROM NORMANDY)

Serves 6 to 8

¾ cup [150 g] short-grain white rice

¾ cup [150 g] sugar

2 teaspoons ground cinnamon

¼ teaspoon ground cardamom (optional)

Scant ¼ teaspoon fine sea salt

1 bay leaf

6 cups [1.4 L] whole milk

1 teaspoon vanilla extract

The name for this cinnamon-laced baked rice pudding comes from the Norman word for "twisted mouth." Depending on which book you reference, the twist of said mouth refers to either the face made when the Normans tasted cinnamon for the first time or when they didn't let their rice pudding cool enough. A modern interpretation could be the face a nonnative speaker makes when trying to pronounce "teurgoule."

Despite the name, the recipe itself is simple and straightforward: Combine rice and cinnamon (two imports that came through Normandy's Honfleur port in the eighteenth century) with whole milk, stir, and bake. After a few hours, a deeply browned top forms to protect the creamy, nearly completely broken-down rice pudding underneath. This is traditionally eaten with a slice of brioche and plenty of dry hard cider, though I say skip the bread but keep the cider flowing.

Preheat the oven to 300°F [150°C].

In an 8- to 10- cup [2 to 2.3 L] ovenproof ceramic baking dish, add the rice, sugar, cinnamon, cardamom (if using), salt, and bay leaf. Stir to combine, then gently pour in the milk and vanilla.

Bake, uncovered, for 1 hour, then lower the heat to 225°F [110°C] and continue to bake until the top is very golden, about 5 hours more. Set aside to cool. Serve at room temperature or chilled.

CRÈME BRÛLÉE

Serves 6

3 cups [720 ml] heavy cream

1 vanilla bean, split and scraped, pod reserved for another use

¼ teaspoon fine sea salt

6 large egg yolks

½ cup [100 g] granulated sugar

Turbinado sugar, for finishing

I knew the woman I was seeing liked me. There were so many clues! Like when she regularly . . . told me how much she liked me. But every single time I cooked something for her, she would say, "C'est pas mal" (literally, "It's not bad"). For a person whose livelihood and some part of her self-worth relies heavily on an ability to cook, consistent lukewarm reviews felt, frankly, pas bien ("not good"). A bit of passive aggression followed by effective communication later. I learned that in French, c'est bon, literally "it's good," is often used to indicate "meh, it's OK" while c'est pas mal ("it's not bad") is more akin to "wow, hey, this is great!" Confusing, right? But there's no confusion in this very classic, very why-fuck-with-something-this-simple-when-it's-this-good dessert because it is extremely pas mal, en fait.

Preheat the oven to 325°F [165°C].

In a medium saucepan over medium-low heat, combine the cream, vanilla bean seeds, and salt and cook until hot but not boiling.

In a medium bowl, whisk together the egg yolks and granulated sugar until lightened in color. Slowly whisk in the hot cream mixture. Strain the custard through a fine-mesh sieve.

Place six ramekins in a large baking dish and divide the custard evenly between the ramekins. Add enough hot water to the baking dish to come halfway up the sides of the ramekins, then bake until the custards are just set, 25 to 40 minutes depending on the height of your ramekins. Carefully remove the ramekins from the water bath and set aside to cool completely. Refrigerate until the custard is completely chilled (at least 4 hours). Covered, they can keep for up to 4 days in the refrigerator.

When you are ready to serve, sprinkle each custard with enough turbinado sugar to fully and evenly cover the top. Use a blowtorch to caramelize each custard by waving the flame over the top until the sugar melts, bubbles, and turns to an even brown caramel. Allow the caramel to harden for about 5 minutes before serving.

MACAROONS

**Makes 24
macaroons**

4¾ cups [285 g] large
flaked unsweetened
coconut

4 large egg whites

1½ teaspoons vanilla
extract

½ teaspoon fine sea salt

¾ cup [150 g] sugar

Note
If you're looking for these in
French bakeries, they're not
the easiest to find, but they
do exist and are called rochers
coco, or "coconut rocks."

There are macarons: pastel, filled, layered, best for tea parties
and those without nut allergies. And there are macaroons:
coconut, toasted, sometimes dipped in chocolate, ideal for
Passover and those with gluten allergies. These are the
latter, almost meringue-like, made to be deeply browned, and
packing big coconut flavor, a.k.a. the way a macaroon should
be but rarely ever is.

Preheat the oven to 350°F [180°C].

Spread the coconut on a baking sheet and toast in the oven
until the flakes start to brown, about 5 minutes. Set aside to
cool slightly.

In a large bowl, combine the egg whites, vanilla, and salt. Whisk
until the egg whites are frothy, 15 to 30 seconds. Whisking
constantly, add the sugar gradually until the mixture is bright
white and thickened (but not so much that peaks form) and
the sugar is completely combined, about 1 minute more. Use a
spatula to fold in the toasted coconut.

Line two rimmed baking sheets with parchment paper.

Using damp hands (to prevent sticking) or a cookie scoop,
gently form the coconut mixture into 1½-inch [4 cm] balls,
each 1½ to 2 tablespoons. Place them on the prepared baking
sheets, leaving about 1 inch [2.5 cm] between the macaroons.

Bake until deeply golden brown, 15 to 20 minutes. Transfer the
macaroons to a cooling rack and let cool completely. Macaroons
can be stored in an airtight container at room temperature for
1 week or in the freezer for up to 3 months.

THE SWEETS PLATE OF YOUR DREAMS

Considering I went to pastry school, it's a slightly dirty secret that an assiette sucrée ("sweet plate") often moonlights as dessert at my gatherings. Don't get me wrong, I love a full dessert, but to me, a combination of sweet-leaning things that look pretty together on a plate is an easy conclusion to a busy day and often more satisfying and accessible after a heavier meal. For the French, this plate is something you put out *after* dessert to keep the night going. To each her own.

With a little grocery shopping foresight, compiling a solid sweets plate can mean simply going into your pantry and grabbing chocolate, nuts, and anything else that looks vaguely company-friendly. Add seasonal fruit and flaky salt, and you're set.

Well, nearly. Not included in the ingredient list below—but essential if you and any of your guests are drinking that night—is a bottle or two of a favorite digestif, a bowl of ice, and a jumble of mismatched glasses. Bonus points if you have a nutcracker you love.

270

ARRANGE EVERYTHING ON A PLATE, ADD A NUTCRACKER, AND SERVE WITH A DIGESTIF.

Serves as many people as you have.

Nuts in the shell, such as walnuts, almonds, pistachios, and hazelnuts

Ripe, in-season fruits, such as nectarines, peaches, plums, apples, watermelon, cantaloupe, and/or figs

Dried fruit, such as figs, dates, apricots, cherries, and/or prunes

Dark and/or milk chocolate, broken into pieces

Assorted cookies, such as Sablés (page 263), Macaroons (page 269), wafers, and/or Thin Mints

Flaky sea salt

FROMAGE!!!

I'm from Wisconsin and I live in Paris, so I'm genetically and contractually obligated to have strong opinions on cheese. Here are some of them:

Americans love to say that the French eat cheese for dessert. Is it true? How best to eat it then? In reality, in France, cheese is not dessert, but you can pretend it is. *Traditionally*, fromage is a course after the meal and before dessert. It's also technically not served before dinner, but that's a rule that's meant to be broken, I say (see page 64).

Just as I have very strong feelings about the number of meats on your plate, board, or slate (see page 99), so too do I have very strong feelings about the number of cheeses on your plate. Three is the number to shoot for here, enough so that one person doesn't hog all the Reblochon, not so many that people can't keep track of what each one is. As you choose your three cheeses, make them different from each other in texture, shape, and milk variety (or all three!) and stop there. This allows your guests the experience of variety without losing out on the fun of going back for multiple tastes of their favorite.

When serving cheese, add salted butter. Make it the best butter you can find, and treat it like a cheese. There are few things more pleasurable than slicing butter the thickness one would slice Brie, spreading it on bread, and then topping it with actual Brie.

Sweet and savory additions to a cheese plate make it clear you care. On the sweet side, fresh and dried fruits, fig spread, and quince paste are great, but have you tried maraschino cherries or a whole honeycomb or a spoonful of caramel? Do. For savory, love me a generous, almost careless handful of mixed olives, cornichons, and mustards, but also what about Pipérade Dip (page 77), kimchi, corn nuts, or a flourish of Cheez-Its? All valid and welcome additions, as long as they suit the cheeses on hand.

Try to have as many utensils on the plate to cut the cheeses as you have cheeses that need to be cut. No hater of blue wants cross-contamination all over their precious triple-crème. Also, should you smartly choose to have a hard-rind cheese like Comté, Mimolette, or something from Spain made of sheep's milk, make it easy on your guests and cut it pre-assembly.

Finally, notice how relentless I've been in calling this a cheese *plate*? Wooden boards and slates are nice but they're not the only surfaces you can put cheese on. I'm partial to long, pretty, oval platters with decorative edges, but anything that's big enough to fit everything on it is a cheese plate in waiting.

DIGESTIFS

APRÈS SPRITZ

For 1

1 ounce [30 ml] Armagnac

1 ounce [30 ml] sweet vermouth

3 ounces [90 ml] dry sparkling Lambrusco

1 ounce [30 ml] soda water

Lemon or orange peel, for garnish

Despite what some may think, I *love* a good spritz. What I don't love is being locked into a certain type of spirit or season or even time of day in order to enjoy the bubbly, refreshing, *ENTIRE CATEGORY* of drink. This particular spritz is written to be served post-meal, preferably as the leaves begin to change and cuffing season takes hold, but that's personal preference. Please think, and drink, for yourself.

In an ice-filled wineglass or lowball glass, combine the Armagnac and vermouth. Top with Lambrusco and soda water. Garnish with a lemon or orange peel and serve.

AMER HIGHBALL + AMER LOWBALL

Note

The bulk of amari you'll find at your local shop come from Italy, and they are excellent. If you're looking for something French and just as excellent, China-China Amer is one of my favorites. If you can find it, enjoy the orange-heavy, complex, and sweet amaro chilled and neat, on the rocks with a twist, or in one of the many amaro drinks in this book.

Just as an apéritif opens the evening and rouses the appetite, a digestif closes the night (or, at least, starts the close of the night, in theory) and helps usher in digestion. Classically, a digestif skews slightly higher in alcohol and is a tad richer and sweeter than your opening drink. Think cognac, Armagnac, Calvados, whiskey, darker sherries, and eau de vie. Bitter—"amer" in French—plays for both teams, however, and you'll often see amari in glasses from sunup to sundown. The Amer Highball is a boozier version of a bitters and soda, while the Amer Lowball is what I would like to drink at the end of every big meal.

AMER HIGHBALL

For 1

2 ounces [60 ml] amaro

3 or 4 dashes Angostura bitters

3 to 4 ounces [90 to 120 ml] club soda

In a highball glass filled with ice, add the amaro and bitters. Top with club soda and serve.

AMER LOWBALL

For 1

1½ ounces [45 ml] blanc vermouth

1½ ounces [45 ml] amaro

2 dashes Angostura bitters

2 lemon peels

2 orange peels

In a mixing glass or shaker filled with ice, combine the vermouth, amaro, and bitters. Hold one lemon peel by its long edges, skin facing down into the mixing glass. Pinch the peel to express the citrus oils and drop it into the glass. Repeat with one of the orange peels. Stir with a cocktail stirrer for 15 seconds, until the cocktail is very cold. Strain into an ice-filled lowball glass, garnish with the remaining citrus peels, and serve.

À CÔTÉ

For 1

1½ ounces [45 ml] cognac

1 ounce [30 ml] orange liqueur

¾ ounce [22.5 ml] fresh lemon juice

Note

To sugar the rim of your cocktail glass, spread superfine sugar on a small plate. Rub a lemon wedge halfway around the rim of your chilled cocktail glass, then dip that side in the sugar to lightly coat the outside rim of the glass.

(Wow, there are just so many accents in the name of this cocktail.) An À Côté is a sidecar, a.k.a. the most underappreciated cocktail of all time. Three ingredients—cognac, orange liqueur, and lemon juice—and no set rule with regard to ratios means you can and should play until you find exactly what you want (also a popular approach to dating). When served as a digestif, I like my À Côtés heavier on the cognac, as written here. If I'm serving a round before sunset, I drop the cognac content to match the orange liqueur and bump up the citrus. Regardless of time of day, I'm a fan of the added texture and kitsch of a sugared half rim, but it's not necessary to the balance of the drink. Serve in chilled tulip glasses or small wineglasses because martini glasses should be outlawed.

In a shaker filled with ice, combine the cognac, orange liqueur, and lemon juice. Cover and shake vigorously. Strain into a chilled tulip glass, small wineglass, or coupe glass and serve.

TONIC TONIC

For 1

1½ ounces [45 ml] oloroso sherry

1½ ounces [45 ml] sweet vermouth

¼ ounce [7.5 ml] fresh lime juice

2 dashes Angostura bitters

Splash of dry tonic water

Tonic water rarely sees its way past apéritif hour, but its digestive powers shine post-meal. Used as an accent rather than a long pour, it adds a quick hit of bubbles and quinine bitterness to oloroso sherry, sweet vermouth, and lime juice. A digestive tonic, with tonic.

In a cocktail shaker filled with ice, combine the sherry, vermouth, lime juice, and bitters. Cover and shake vigorously. Strain into an ice-filled lowball glass, top with a splash of tonic, and serve.

GOÛTE MOI

For 1

1½ ounces [45 ml] Calvados

1½ ounces [45 ml]
Dubonnet Rouge

3 dashes orange bitters

Sparkling wine, for topping

This is the drink to serve when you're trying to seduce (with enthusiastic consent). The strength of the Calvados is smoothed over with an equal amount of Dubonnet, and it provides an excuse to pop open something bubbly post-dinner. If none of that works, the name translates to "taste me." You know what, actually, just lead with that.

In an ice-filled mixing glass or shaker, combine the Calvados, Dubonnet, and bitters. Stir with a cocktail stirrer for 15 seconds, until the cocktail is very cold. Strain into a coupe glass, top with sparkling wine, and serve.

BRAVO, VOUS AVEZ GAGNÉ

For 1

2 ounces [60 ml] Calvados

Overflowing ¼ ounce
1:1 simple syrup (see Note,
page 36)

3 dashes orange bitters

Orange peel

A favorite store-bought French treat is a box of light, crispy, cream-filled wafer cookies. They're reminiscent of those brightly and artificially colored and flavored treats from (my) American childhood. You know the ones. They were terrible. This drink has nothing to do with them other than the fact that the first time I made it I was snacking on the aforementioned French cookie equivalent (which are embossed with little sayings) and now can only associate it with them. For those who don't have or want that association, think of it as an old-fashioned made with Calvados. Either way, vous avez gagné ("you win").

In an ice-filled mixing glass or shaker, combine the Calvados, simple syrup, and bitters. Stir with a cocktail stirrer for 15 seconds, until the cocktail is very cold. Strain into an ice-filled lowball glass. Hold the orange peel by its long edges, skin facing down into the glass. Pinch the peel to express the citrus oils, drop the peel into the glass, and serve.

BONAL AFTER HOURS

For 4

3 ounces [90 ml] Bonal

2 ounces [60 ml] dry vermouth

½ ounce [15 ml] orange liqueur

4 dashes Angostura bitters

2 orange peels

Note

Bonal is a lightly bitter, floral, fortified apéritif wine made with gentian root, cinchona bark, and herbs. The bottle is, like many French apéritif bottles, beautiful in a classic kind of way. If you can't find it, sub out the Bonal for another bitter-leaning, lower-ABV bottle like Punt e Mes or Dubonnet and call it "_____ After Hours."

Not shots, not full-size cocktails, these are to be served when you want to show off those too-small-for-wine, too-big-for-single-pours, pretty little flea market glasses you love and never use.

In an ice-filled mixing glass or shaker, combine the Bonal, vermouth, orange liqueur, and bitters. Hold an orange peel by its long edges, skin facing down into the glass. Pinch the peel to express the citrus oils, and drop the peel into the glass. Repeat with the second orange peel. Stir with a cocktail stirrer for 15 seconds, until the cocktail is very cold. Divide between four small glasses and serve.

PARIS X NEW YORK

For 1

1¼ ounces [35 ml] rye whiskey or bourbon

1 ounce [30 ml] sweet vermouth

½ ounce [15 ml] dry vermouth

¼ ounce [7.5 ml] eau de vie, such as cherry, apple, quince, or pear

2 or 3 dashes Angostura bitters

2 very good maraschino cherries, for garnish

I had my first Manhattan in my early twenties shortly after moving to Manhattan. Many moons and a move to Paris later, it's still my wintertime drink of choice—and I still make sure there's an extra snacking cherry tucked into the glass. This variation is an ode to those East Village nights, but for Paris, in my thirties.

In an ice-filled mixing glass or shaker, combine the whiskey, sweet vermouth, dry vermouth, eau de vie, and bitters. Stir with a cocktail stirrer for 15 seconds, until the cocktail is very cold. Pour into a small wineglass or coupe glass, garnish with the cherries, and serve.

MERCI BIEN

For 1

1½ ounces [45 ml] cognac

¾ ounce [22.5 ml] sweet vermouth

¼ ounce [7.5 ml] allspice dram

¼ ounce [7.5 ml] fresh orange juice

1 maraschino cherry, for garnish

One of the best and also worst things about dating in another language is, well, learning another language. "Merci bien" genuinely means "thank you very much," but when said in one of my French ex's Parisian accent and with a bit of sass, it can easily become an extremely sarcastic version of "thank you very much." She was actually super hot and nice. It didn't work out. It's fine. Everyone's fine.

In a cocktail shaker filled with ice, combine the cognac, vermouth, allspice dram, and orange juice. Cover and shake vigorously. Add a cherry to the bottom of a coupe glass, strain the mixture into the glass, and serve.

BOOZY FRUIT FOR WOMEN+

Makes 1 pound [455 g]

1 pound [455 g] large prunes (about 3 cups), unpitted

1 vanilla bean, split and scraped

3 tablespoons sugar

2 cups [480 ml] Armagnac or Bas Armagnac

I've been told that way back when, before it was deemed "OK" for women to drink the same way men drink—please don't get me started—eating a piece or two of fruit soaked in sugar and alcohol was considered a proper alternative. Considering each of the following is akin to taking a shot, I'd say whoever was eating these was *quite* capable of handling their alcohol. These particular booze-soaked fruits are a specialty in southwestern France where Gascony's Armagnac (a regional brandy) meets sticky, plump, sweet prunes from the town of Agen (which borders Gascony). The longer the prunes sit, the smoother the flavor becomes. Use cognac or Calvados if you can't find Armagnac, add more prunes as your stash gets low, eat plain or with crème fraîche or over ice cream, and for the love of deconstructing the gender binary, serve them to everyone on the spectrum.

Combine the prunes, vanilla bean pod, and vanilla seeds in a large, clean jar. In a small saucepan over medium heat, combine ⅓ cup [80 ml] of water and the sugar. Bring to a boil, stirring until the sugar dissolves. Pour over the prunes and set aside to cool to room temperature. Add the Armagnac, making sure the liquid completely covers the prunes, and stir to combine. Tightly cover and refrigerate for at least 2 weeks before serving. Continue adding prunes as they are eaten. The soaked prunes will keep almost infinitely in the refrigerator.

DIGESTIF SHOTS

One might associate the word "shot" with a now-closed dive bar, drunken 3 a.m. rounds pressed into hands by that one friend (they were an Aries, weren't they), and hazy memories of possibly poor decisions. Associate no more. Digestif shots exist on the low-ABV/brilliant quadrant of the matrix and offer an ideal conclusion to whatever variety of night you've had . . . or segue to the night you are looking to have, should you be the type of person to go out after dinner.

Instead of straight booze slammed over dessert, digestif shots are fast-moving, miniature cocktails that lean heavily on lower-ABV aromatized wine- and spirit-based bottles and favor, if you have some, vintage glassware over souvenir kiosk shot glasses with, say, the Eiffel tower etched on them.

Since these are multifaceted drinks in and of themselves, you could be tempted to make each digestif shot as a full-size cocktail. Please don't. Instead, raise a petite verre to the deeper reason shots of any kind are the most fun: They bind us together in the fleeting joy of the present, one round at a time.

So, just because it's not nearing bar close, the floor isn't sticky, or you've been in therapy long enough to hold back on any self-sabotaging decisions doesn't mean there shouldn't be someone out there wrangling the group together for shots. That person, in fact, can and should be you.

DIGESTIF SHOT UN

Makes eight 1½-ounce [45 ml] shots

4 ounces [120 ml] dry gin

4 ounces [120 ml] fino sherry

4 ounces [120 ml] dry vermouth

Green olives for eating after shooting

In an ice-filled mixing glass or shaker, combine the gin, sherry, and vermouth. Stir with a cocktail stirrer for 15 seconds, until the cocktail is very cold. Strain into shot glasses. Serve with olives.

DIGESTIF SHOT DEUX

Makes eight 1½-ounce [45 ml] shots

8 ounces [240 ml] Picon

2½ ounces [80 ml] sweet vermouth

1½ ounces [45 ml] fresh lemon juice

10 dashes orange bitters

In a shaker filled with ice, combine the Picon, vermouth, lemon juice, and bitters. Cover and shake vigorously. Strain into shot glasses and serve.

DIGESTIF SHOT TROIS

Makes eight 1½-ounce [45 ml] shots

4 ounces [120 ml] amaro, such as China-China

4 ounces [120 ml] red bitter, such as Campari or Cappelletti

4 ounces [120 ml] sweet vermouth

Orange peel

In an ice-filled mixing glass or shaker, combine the amaro, red bitter, and vermouth. Hold the orange peel by its long edges, skin facing down into the glass. Pinch the peel to express the citrus oils, and drop the peel into the glass. Stir with a cocktail stirrer for 15 seconds, until the cocktail is very cold. Strain into shot glasses and serve.

DIGESTIF SHOT QUATRE

Makes eight 1½-ounce [45 ml] shots

6 ounces [180 ml] cognac

3 ounces [90 ml] fresh orange juice

1½ ounces [45 ml] orgeat

1½ ounces [45 ml] orange liqueur

6 dashes Angostura bitters

In a shaker filled with ice, combine the cognac, orange juice, orgeat, orange liqueur, and bitters. Cover and shake vigorously. Strain into shot glasses and serve.

A TAKEAWAY ON TAKEAWAYS

Remember goodie bags at kid's birthday parties? Regardless of the fact that they were often a cheap, gendered toy or stale candy necklace, I loved the added bonus of going to a party *and* getting a present to take home. As adults, we sometimes get these take-home treats in the form of a box of Jordan almonds at the end of a wedding, but it doesn't quite hit the same. When I started wrapping little, individual edible gifts for my guests to take home at the end of a dinner, I realized how easy it is to tap back into that simple, childlike joy. A little cookie wrapped in parchment or granola (see following) tucked into a small takeaway box (unused! you can get these at a paper goods store or online) and marked with a guest's name extends the sweetness of an already great dinner party into the following day. While I don't do it all the time, when I do send a takeaway home with guests, I'm never sorry. The key is to make sure it's something easily made in advance so you're not bothered with another thing day of. Sablés but Not, Like, Regular Sablés, Cool Sablés (page 263), Thibault's Madeleines (page 264), and Macaroons (page 269) are all choice takeaways (and I'm all for furthering the cookies-for-breakfast cause), but here's another recipe that feels like a slightly healthier pre–10 a.m. choice.

GRANOLA

Preheat the oven to 325°F [165°C]. In a large bowl, combine 4 cups [400 g] of old-fashioned rolled oats, 2 cups [280 g] of raw, whole pecans, 1 cup [60 g] of large flaked unsweetened coconut, ⅔ cup [160 g] of coconut oil (melted), ½ cup [120 ml] of pure maple syrup, ½ cup [100 g] of dark brown sugar, 1 tablespoon of vanilla extract, 3 tablespoons of poppy seeds, 3 tablespoons of sesame seeds, 2 teaspoons of flaky sea salt, 1½ teaspoons of ground cinnamon, and a pinch of ground cloves. Stir until completely combined, then spread on a rimmed baking sheet and bake until golden brown, stirring every 10 minutes or so. It should take 40 to 50 minutes total. Cool completely before dividing among disposable containers.

ACKNOWLEDGMENTS

When I moved to Paris in 2015, I didn't know a single person inside the borders of France. Today, the folks who regularly gather à table—locals and visitors alike—are among the greatest I've known anywhere. I'm thankful to the city that brought us together—and the butter and wine that keep us here.

I am incredibly lucky to surround myself with smart women and call it work. Three such women joined me on the ground to create the images in these pages. Joann Pai, the moment we started shooting Book 1, I knew we were going to make Book 2. Your eye for light and form and your hunger for Seven-Hour Leg of Lamb remain unmatched. Thank you for letting me bottle a bit more of your gifts in these pages. C'est un rêve de travailler avec toi. Lina Caschetto, stylist, assistant, and friend extraordinaire, merci mille fois for your countless hours in and out of various kitchens, brocantes, and marchés across France. And merci infiniment for making the kouign-amann again and again and again and again, laughing on my kitchen floor when we could have been crying, and then nailing it. Kate Devine, I still can't believe that in the middle of your doctoral thesis you agreed to also photo assist this book. Grateful for you in so many ways, not least of all because living down the street from you feels like living down the street from family.

The people who regularly gather à table chez moi are also many of the people you see gathering in the pages of *À Table*. Thibault Charpentier, Yasmin Zeinab, Jackie Kai Ellis, Lucie Camara, Katy Yung, Natanya Bravo, and Roxanne Matiz: I am forever indebted to you for lending your faces and bodies and hearts to this book and my life—come over Sunday?

To the friends whose faces you won't see here but who spent the better part of a year gathering around real and proverbial tables in Paris, Provence, Los Angeles, and New York City as I developed and tested and retested (and retested) these recipes, thank you for your love and your appetites, your considered feedback and support. Deep, intimate, cross-continental relationships are beyond challenging to maintain and I thank you each of you for putting in the energy to keep the love alive. Alexis deBoschnek, Jade Zimmerman, Kort Havens, Ryan Hanke, Jamie Feldmar, Ben Mims, J Anderson, Susan Korn, Emily Fiffer, Heather Sperling, Dayna Evans, Lindsey Tramuta, Yvonne Kawamura, Katie Quinn, Tessa Stuart, Erin Hartigan, Be Shakti, and Liz Clayman, this book and the person who wrote it would not exist without you.

To Cindy Davis, my therapist in Paris who picked up where the aforementioned people left off (and thus allowed my friendships with them to carry through) and who continues to push me through all the work, including but certainly not limited to that of an expat in a system built to weed out all but the most persistent, thank you, thank you, thank you.

Blake W. MacKay, to share so much love, history, and respect both personally and professionally with a person is rare and hard-won in this—and many other—lives. It's an honor and a privilege to navigate that particular magic with you. Thank you for seeing me and my writing more clearly than I could sometimes see myself and helping me bring and share this deuxième livre into and with the world. Let's make another.

To my goddaughter, light of my life, Peridot Zimmerman, who came to Paris for the first time while I was writing this book, thank you for letting me newly see and newly fall for this city through your eyes; I can't wait to do it again. Also, thank you for reminding me that Cheez-Its very much do belong on cheese boards.

The tables and balconies and mantels featured in these pages are real places here in France and I'm lucky to call one of them home and others homes away from home. Paul and Sharon Mrozinski, your apartment in Bonnieux makes a girl want to run away to the Luberon. Kate Devine and Vincent David, the cover (and plenty of other images) wouldn't exist without you and your beautiful home. Christine Muhlke, your Paris apartment is a refuge the likes of which I never even dreamed. Raising a glass to you, especially.

I sourced many of the props from brocantes and flea markets and little vintage shops all over France. When I didn't, I leaned on Ivy Weinglass and Astier de Villatte for some insane ceramics, Victoire Taverne for custom embroidery, and Yumiko Sekine at Fog Linen Work for the most beautiful linens. Also a hearty thank-you to ARCH THE, La Double J, and Nikki Chasin, among others, for the threads.

To so many others across France (and beyond) who aided in my eating and drinking in the name of research: Joanna and Laurent at Distillerie Cazottes; Paul Caillouel at Domaine Sicera; Cyril Zang; Lise Kvan and Eric Montéléon at Le Saint Hubert in Saint-Saturnin-lès-Apt; Valentin Letoquart at Val de Combrès; Jean-François + family at Calvados Michel Huard; Isabelle and Aurelie Kayser, Quentin Chapuis, and many more, thank you. Erin Sylvester and Megan Krigbaum, you are my wine intel heroes representing in LA and NYC, respectively. Thank you for making sure I was meeting the right producers, drinking the right "research" bottles, and putting accurate information into these pages.

À TABLE

Sarah Smith, ma agente et amie, thank you for listening to my dreams and helping (sometimes pushing) me to make them realities. Thank you, also, for not too infrequently playing the role of therapist with such compassion and tact. Please don't switch jobs but know that you very well could.

Sarah Billingsley, working with you and the Chronicle team has been everything one hopes for as an author. Thank you for listening, affirming, and pushing me to shape this text into something that feels like the best version of myself à table. Lizzie Vaughan, my incredible designer, never in my life have I loosely described what I would like to see and had it delivered both perfectly and far better than I could have imagined or put into words. Thank you. Thanks also to Claire Gilhuly, Magnolia Molcan, Steve Kim, Tera Killip, Cynthia Shannon, and Joyce Lin.

To my beautiful, smart, and relentlessly supportive mother, Diane. It's not enough to dedicate a recipe or book to you. You created a rock-solid foundation for my love of words and food and a firmer-than-rock-solid support system when that love took me an ocean away. Thank you for believing in and visiting me (Mike, you too!) wherever I choose to call home.

Finally, to Paris. For so many things but especially for being the city I came to in order to discover my truest self. You are the city where I came out, where I wrote my first book and now my second, where I learned to love sea snails and also myself. In much the same line of thought: to the women both in Paris and not whom I've loved for a little or long time, you helped shape me and thus, this life. Merci, merci, merci.

Just as in life, our tables are often a mix of gratitude, exhaustion, anticipation, anxiety, trust, miscommunication, laughter, and—if we're lucky—a whole lot of love. The tables, recipes, and stories in these pages are an attempt to capture the enchanted, jumbled, sometimes sexy, always delicious reality that is home cooking and gathering in France. C'est un honneur de partager un peu de cette magie avec vous. Merci à toutes. / It's an honor to share a bit of that magic with you. Thank you all.

—RP

INDEX

À TABLE

À TABLE